D0681297

What Big Ears You Have!

What Big Ears You Have!

The Theologians' Red Riding Hood

Otto Hermann Pesch

Translated by
Grant Kaplan
and
Linda M. Maloney

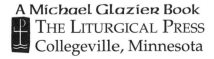

A Michael Glazier Book
THE LITURGICAL PRESS
Collegeville, Minnesota

A Michael Glazier Book published by The Liturgical Press.

Cover design by Ann Blattner. Illustration by Barbara Bedrisch-Bos from *"Meine wunderbare Märchenwelt" – Die 20 schönsten Märchen der Brüder Grimm.* Used with permission.

What Big Ears You Have! was originally published in Germany by Verlag Herder GmbH & Co. KG © Verlag Herder im Breisgau 1998 under the title *Warum hast du so grosse Ohren?*

© 2000 by The Order of St. Benedict, Inc., Collegeville, Minnesota. All rights reserved. No part of this book may be reproduced in any form or by any means, electronic or mechanical, including photocopying, recording, taping, or any retrieval system, without the written permission of The Liturgical Press, Collegeville, Minnesota 56321. Printed in the United States of America.

1   2   3   4   5   6   7   8

Library of Congress Cataloging-in-Publication Data

Pesch, Otto Hermann.
    [Warum hast du so grosse Ohren. English]
    What big ears you have! : the theologians' Red Riding Hood / Otto Hermann Pesch ; translated by Grant Kaplan.
        p.   cm.
    ISBN 0-8146-5898-9 (alk. paper)
    1. Theology. 2. Little Red Riding Hood (Tale)   I. Title.

BR118.P45   2000
230—dc21

                                         00-021134

To my family:
Marianne, Winfried, and their "houses";
In memory of my brother Albert;
and in the hope
that we may see more humor in the Church.

Contents

Once Upon a Time There
Was a Theology Department

Once upon a time there was a theology department. Whether it was Catholic or Protestant is not important, nor need anyone know. Men and women lived and worked in harmony in this department. There were tenured and untenured professors (the department lacked woman professors for a long time, a fact that everyone lamented, but thank goodness that has changed), graduate students and visiting scholars of both genders, male and female undergraduates and librarians, female administrators and secretaries (male administrators were a paucity, and men were totally absent from the secretarial ranks, which almost nobody lamented). At times they disagreed quite vociferously with one another, not just the tenured professors among themselves, but also with the untenured, the professors with the graduate students, the graduate students among themselves and with the undergraduates, administrators with secretaries, the secretaries with the professors, the women undergraduates with the men, and both among themselves and with everyone else (except for the administrators and secretaries). They argued about their scholarship, about university politics, about things in general and about global injustice both *in abstracto* and *in concreto.* But every disagreement was followed by a reconciliation. Sometimes department members quarreled vigorously in the morning and attended festive gatherings together in the evening. For this reason, both within the university and among other theology departments this department was greatly admired.

There was only one weakness in this department, actually a weakness of many other departments as well: the inevitable meetings of task forces and committees. These were prescribed by the university, and took up an inordinate amount of time. The reason lay in the fact that everything had to be decided democratically, and therefore everyone had to be allowed to voice his or her opinion freely before anything could come to a vote. It is well known that dictatorial decisions save time, and democracy takes longer. Hence impatience swelled in many department members, especially when all the arguments and counter-arguments had been stated, and the discussion still continued.

There was one professor who was especially impatient, and he found the long meetings painfully tedious. How he would have loved to be sitting instead at his desk with a theological book or a manuscript! But he attended the meetings out of a sense of obligation. He pondered how he could make this wasted time more useful. First he tried to read, but he could not concentrate. Then he attempted to write letters, but most letters needed to be written on his PC, and obviously he could not do so during meetings.

He heard about a colleague who for similar reasons wrote stories during the meetings. This did not require much concentration; one only needed to "tune out" what was said, not a difficult task during a typically dull meeting. Meanwhile, at conferences or over a glass of wine in the evening, the professor several times heard a retelling of the famous fairy tale of Little Red Riding Hood in the inimitably beautiful language of German bureaucracy. It took some effort to secure a copy of the text. Perhaps you are not familiar with it? It goes something like this:

> In the juvenile sector of our township there is record of a certain resident minor not yet of school age, who through her unusual headdress became known in common usage as Little Red Riding Hood. Because of the fact that she did not pay heed to the requirements [of her mother] she committed a punishable offense, and during her violation of the official ban on picking flowers she met a not-officially-registered wolf without permanent residence. In blatant disregard for the law, this wolf demanded to be allowed to examine the basket container designed for the

transportation of consumable goods. Since a deficiency prevailed on the part of the wolf in the realm of nutrition, the wolf arrived at the decision to misrepresent himself before R.'s grandmother through the submission of falsified papers. . . . The official in charge of the forest, while proceeding on his course of duty, heard the sound of snarling and identified the source of this snarling as being located at the mouth of the animal. . . . Through their unexpected resuscitation both persons acquired an increased, although officially illegal sense of levity, to which they gave expression through disorderly conduct, loud noise creating a public nuisance, and disregard of other police procedures, which necessarily led to their arrest. The incident was recorded through the culturally promotional activity of the Grimm brothers, and made available as a fairy tale for families with an endowment of children numbering in significant figures. . . .

And so on. Quite mysteriously the text, copied from a typewritten manuscript, did not give the name of the author. Allegedly a colleague from the legal field had invented the story. Only later did the professor learn that the story derived from Thaddäus Troll.[1] However that may be, the story-scribbling colleague and the "bureaucratic" Little Red Riding Hood sparked the imagination of the theology professor. How would the story of Little Red Riding Hood sound if he wrote it in the language of *his* field, systematic theology? He made his attempt without any trepidation and thus experienced one of the most pleasant department meetings in his professional career.

But *dared* he do so without any trepidation? Was it proper to make jokes with words and concepts that are usually reserved for the expression of sacred topics: God, Jesus Christ, the Holy Spirit, the Gospel, the grace of God, eternal life, and many other such matters? Wasn't the professor committing a sin against the Second Commandment, the one that earlier generations of Catholic school children were questioned about in their books for examination of conscience: "Did I take the Lord's name in vain?"

1. See Postscript, p. 79.

Nevertheless, the professor thought of two good reasons for the propriety of such a task. First of all, he came from Cologne, and it is well known that people from Cologne do not take anything quite seriously except for God alone. How should he take seriously a theology derived from humans and not from God? Second, he was deeply imbued with the truth that the apostle Paul expressed: "For we know only in part, and we prophesy only in part; but when the complete comes, the partial will come to an end. . . . For now we see in a mirror, dimly, but then we will see face to face" (1 Cor 13:9, 12). Whenever he read these lines from Sacred Scripture he thought to himself: we theologians, especially the men, are always in danger of forgetting the provisional and temporal nature of our work. Although we surely become wise through the study of theology, we are continually succumbing to the temptation to suppose that our minuscule thoughts or our grand constructive concepts can mirror the actual thought of God. The more we devote ourselves to the task with zeal and passion, the greater our fall into error. What antidote can one take against this chronic theological sickness?

If the study of the history of theology is not powerful enough, if the sight of all the theological theories that have landed in the rubbish heap of history does not make enough of an impression, perhaps one should try derision, friendly derision, of course. So poor Little Red Riding Hood must suffer in order to chide theology, or as one says in the professor's home town of Cologne, to "pull its leg."

But why Little Red Riding Hood? Could one not just as well perform some "theological leg pulling" with the fairy tale of Snow White, or with the troll and the seven goats, or with the frog prince? Of course one could. Inspired by the example of the "bureaucratic" text, the professor most likely did not even consider other options, and stuck with Little Red Riding Hood. Besides, this fairy tale was especially suited for the task because, until the very end, it is such an ordinary story, whereas the other fairy tales are full of marvels from the very beginning. But perhaps someone else will attempt the same thing with Snow White. . . .

The fairy tale of the theology department and the professor could end here. One day the government passed a new law for higher education that called for a reduction of the numbers of those required for meetings. Naturally there was a reduction in the number of requests to speak during the meetings. From one day to the next the meetings no longer lasted six to eight hours, but instead two to three. Now everyone needed to listen intently; there was no more time for writing stories. But the fairy tale went on. Somehow the students learned that a theological version of Little Red Riding Hood was floating around. At that time the faculty used to stage a weekend presentation to conclude the orientation week for new students at the beginning of each semester. It ended with, what else, a party! And so that the first-year students could take home a proper impression of theology for their future study, the organizers of the weekend requested that the professor read his "Little Red Riding Hood: A Systematic Theology" at the party. Everyone enjoyed the reading, and they showed their approval with peals of laughter—although the first-year students could hardly understand any of the technical jargon. The next year the organizers of the orientation week asked the professor for another "fairy tale hour." He composed a new story of Little Red Riding Hood, so as not to repeat himself, this time giving rise to "Little Red Riding Hood: A Theological Propaedeutic." And in the following year there was "Little Red Riding Hood: A Church History," since church history was the subject closest to the professor's own field.

Meanwhile the students in the department had started a newsletter. They asked the now notorious inventor of fairy tales if they could print the different versions of Little Red Riding Hood. The storyteller could hardly say no, but now he was in a bind. In the following semesters he had to invent new variations of Little Red Riding Hood in the jargon of all the theological disciplines, right up to the "Epilogue in Heaven." Oh, how he rejoiced when he finally finished! He learned that it is sometimes easier to write a theological article than a story. And he also learned that one had only mastered a theological discipline when one could play games with the "technical jargon" for some healthy theological ridicule. Hence he could not and dared not resist the temptation to pull the proverbial leg of his dear colleagues, with whom he got along so well.

At this point the fairy tale of the theology department and the professor would have come to a close had not a man arrived one day who held an influential position with a famous and powerful German publisher. This man already had a good relationship with the professor, and explained that he, too, had heard something about a "theological" Little Red Riding Hood. He asked for the manuscript, found it enjoyable, showed it to other colleagues at the publisher, and recommended that the stories be published as a book. The professor was delighted and agreed with the proposal. He wanted to publish the stories under a pseudonym, however, but one which would easily betray the correct name. He wanted this also for the names of the colleagues whom he named in the stories. The publishers found this somewhat cowardly. Besides, they thought quite correctly that it would be very helpful for the book and the whole project if readers knew right away who this cynic was who "pulled the leg" of his own discipline. The professor reasoned to himself: in a few years my career will come to an end, and this can't do much damage to my future, so why not?

So it came to be that the storyteller gave his own name, but designated his colleagues with code names, a puzzle for the curious, but not too difficult. Thus the fairy tale of the theology department is really ended, and you, dear readers, hold the result in your hands, with three more stories for the new edition. And if the people on this faculty have not passed away, they are still alive. They live in fact today, as joyful, peaceful, and eager to engage in debate as ever. And when they pass away, this book, lying dust-covered in some library, will still give some information about them:

Once upon a time there was a theology department, where poor Little Red Riding Hood was to receive her theological due . . .

Little Red Riding Hood:
A Systematic Theology

There once existed a young individual of that class of creatures who are distinguished in Gen 1:27 as an alternative variety (gender) of that being produced on the sixth day of creation and called "Adam." Since the creature to whom this story pertains regularly wore a red hat—a present from its grandmother—there was, from the standpoint of a hermeneutics of signification, no reason why she should not be called "Little Red Riding Hood."

Little Red Riding Hood "ex-isted," that is to say, as distinct from all that is merely "present," she projected her being ever anew into the future. When the *Kairos* came, her parents, appealing to the Fourth Commandment (according to both Lutheran and Catholic numeration), sent her with the commission to render to her grandmother the service of neighborly love and to care for her with food and drink in the light of Matt 25:31-46. To that end, Little Red Riding Hood had to follow a path through an accumulation of the creatures formed on the third day, which, when standing close together in especially great numbers, are called a "forest" in the common language of our communities. Her parents thus "put" Little Red Riding Hood "under the word" and said: "In the order of salvation there is only *one* way to grandmother's. If you turn from it, disaster, death, and the wrath of God await you!"

Little Red Riding Hood allowed herself to be encountered existentially by the kerygma, and decided on its essentiality by clinging to the word of her parents purely *ex auditu* without any need of further substantiation. She took the *signa efficacia* (efficient signs) of neighborly love, integrated them into a basket, and went on her way in full present-eschatological confidence.

However, the experiences of temptation could not remain absent. Little Red Riding Hood's existential identity was subjected to an increasing threat that gave every occasion to reflect upon the basic human "existential" of "concern." This threat reached its apex when a certain animal appeared who, as everyone knows, and as I can regard as established by exegesis, goes by the name of "wolf." He asked Little Red Riding Hood about the immanent *finis ultimus* (ultimate purpose) of her journey, and Little Red Riding Hood gave a practical-theological analysis of her intentions. Achieving immediate existential satisfaction from this information, the wolf reached a rational conclusion and devised a plan. He convinced Little Red Riding Hood to take a systematic excursus in the flowers and grounded the necessity of this activity by appealing to the structural plausibility of thus attaining the optimal systematic construction of her program of visitation.

Little Red Riding Hood appropriated the wolf's conception as her own without reflecting analytically on, let alone comprehending, the implicit, dangerous consequences thereof. As a result the wolf was able to escape unhindered from the context of the argument. Further, he had at his disposal the most proficient practical-theoretical approach for yielding to his anthropologically unintegrable *appetitus naturalis sensitivus* (in plain language, his appetite) and for devouring the grandmother in a sound methodological manner before Little Red Riding Hood, diverted by her horticultural excursus, finally arrived at her grandmother's house.

Unlike the parousia of Christ, this situation was obviously not deferred for long: Little Red Riding Hood appeared, or, to explicate precisely in the terminology of systematic theology, the "event of being" took place at the house of the grandmother. That is to say, she presenced in a manner devoid of analogy as the multidimensional being-there that distinguishes human existence. Little Red Riding Hood, identical with herself in the naïveté whose innocence renders one incapable of perceiving a foreign non-identity, attempted to actualize a portion of dialogical existence, and involved the wolf, who she thought was her grandmother, in a discourse absent of any power structure on the specific difference between animal and human bodily organs. They spoke of ears, eyes, hands, and mouth, or more precisely, muzzle and teeth. The terms "muzzle" and "teeth" were of that excellent sort of concepts of communication theory that, when spoken, have the performative capacity to effect the transition from an abstract theory of action to concrete action itself: thus Little Red Riding Hood participated in the fate of her grandmother.

At this point I must insert a decisive comment, suited perfectly to shed light with the utmost precision on the differences between the perspectives of the purely secular or philosophical sciences and the theological perspective on the human fate, i.e., death. Every non-theological view of death must end in hopeless aporias of futility, the literal an-nihilation of the entirety of human meaning, or as the case may be, the dynamic of our human questioning. Only theology has the power to testify that the sum of human meaning is not destroyed in death, but instead preserved and saved in eschatological finality; yes, I venture to say that it is "lifted up," "elevated," *"aufgehoben"* in the Hegelian sense.

It must therefore be concluded that Little Red Riding Hood's diaconal actions were not reduced to absurdity by her gruesome death; rather, these actions thereby achieved eschatological definition. A thoroughly transhistorical character was attached to her death and to the death of the grandmother.

On the historical side of the infinite qualitative difference between time and eternity, the soteriological connection became manifest through the appearance of the hunter. He recognized the deadly, egocentric self-confinement of the wolf by his snarl, opened (unclosed) the wolf's stomach, and thus *dis*-closed to Little Red Riding Hood and her grandmother the transition to a new life.

Little Red Riding Hood and the grandmother are thus shown to be paradigmatic figures representing the totality of human meaning transcending time and history, in which death and life, pain and joy, death and resurrection, action and reception, freedom and grace, kerygma and myth, existence and essence, individuality and sociality are dialectically mediated and yet paradoxically identical—that totality of human meaning, if I may so formulate it in conclusion, that is always prehended in the darkness of human questioning and *ap*-prehended in the dim light of faith, but is only *com*-prehended in the bright daylight of systematic-theological reflection. Let the reader understand (see Matt 24:15)!

Little Red Riding Hood:
A Theological Propaedeutic

Once upon a time there was a first-year student who perceived in herself certain motivational structures to make reflected Christian practice into a life project. Her parents noticed this and decided to guide her in a practically oriented propaedeutical course. What was more appropriate than to allow the young woman to experience the fundamental propaedeutical question, "To what purpose faith and religion?" in its existential relevance in the context of a Christian deed? As an indication of the new existential initiative and as a sign of her confessional identity, her parents fitted her with a red hood—donated by her grandmother—and henceforth called her "Little Red Riding Hood." The task given to Little Red Riding Hood, without any performance-oriented pressure, was as follows: to bring cake and wine to her grandmother, who lived in the forest. For curricular reasons the young woman was not allowed to stray from the path, and had to that extent to accept a certain tie to the propaedeutic instructors, that is to say, her parents ("relationship to the director"). Above all, she was not to enter on any other plan of study, since nobody except her parents had mastered the propaedeutic style of her instruction with sufficiently reflected deliberation.

Little Red Riding Hood laid all prior distractions aside and readied herself. She embraced the task at hand and set out by a sure method on her way. While she was underway she had an encounter that greatly disturbed her initial security of orientation: A wolf appeared and involved Little Red Riding Hood in a conversation that confused the thematically centered, propaedeutic approach to the exercise assigned by the parents in such a way that she was unable to set things aright. The wolf insinuated that Little Red Riding Hood should, so to speak as an intermediate unit before completion of the curricular task, leave the path to pick flowers and bring them to the grandmother. Little Red Riding Hood did not perceive that in the wolf's strategy this was aimed at a perfect manipulation of the propaedeutic orientation of Little Red Riding Hood, indeed at a total functional inversion of the propaedeutic arrangement as a whole. Thus the wolf, unnoticed by Little Red Riding Hood, was able to reach the grandmother's house first.

As the wolf knocked on the door, the grandmother inserted an orientation unit and asked who was at the door. The wolf veiled his true identity and answered in a hushed voice that Little Red Riding Hood was at her door with cake and wine. At this the grandmother overcame all problems of communication and intersubjective friction and told the wolf to press down the door handle. The rest is well known: not much later, the wolf had overwhelmed the grandmother; that is to say, he devoured her, and thus robbed Little Red Riding Hood of the object of her propaedeutic exercise.

Little Red Riding Hood was not supposed to find this out immediately; hence the wolf disguised himself, and as Little Red Riding Hood arrived he entered upon some role-playing in which he himself played the role of the grandmother quite convincingly. An intensively instructive conversational unit followed in which the wolf was able to answer all of the young woman's questions about ears, eyes, hands, and teeth without any lingering feelings of frustration. The conditions for a theme-centered interaction on the basis of a theological-anthropological exercise would have been met if the wolf had not departed from his role at the sound of the word "teeth," and devoured Little Red Riding Hood, thus anticipating, so to speak, what should have been a posterior task.

Thus the original propaedeutic intention for Little Red Riding Hood was transformed into a highly relevant existential situation: the wolf had fully and completely realized his intended inversion, and at this point Little Red Riding Hood had to say to herself that theological propaedeutic had instead become the gravest of theological situations. Because of the premature interruption of the propaedeutic phase, our student was most poorly prepared for this situation, and thus a temporary phase of mere passivity in the learning process could not be avoided. The urgency of the situation simply overpowered the sum total of methodological preparation that had already been attained.

As the parents, lacking any advantage in information concerning the turn of events, were unable to provide effective propaedeutical assistance, a change in leadership was required, and it succeeded because, just in time, it became possible to add the hunter to the team of docents. This hunter, from the outset skeptical of exaggerated methodical planning, did not at first attempt to motivate Little Red Riding Hood to her own activity, but instead enacted an authoritative incision in the stomach of the wolf and retrieved Little Red Riding Hood, still completely passive, as well as the grandmother, who was indispensable for the continuation of the instructional task. Thus was the original propaedeutic situation for learning restored, and all immediately began its evaluation at a shared meal of cake and wine. The wolf, on the other hand, was excluded from any kind of further cooperation in the propaedeutic exercise.

Indeed, the radical contact with reality that had happened to Little Red Riding Hood external to any curricular planning (one would not venture to say that this would replace a course in eschatology), considerably accelerated Little Red Riding Hood's learning process. Soon it was obvious that the young woman no longer needed to be saddled with the whole package of propaedeutic assignments, and every propaedeutic phase was no longer necessary. Little Red Riding Hood soon took her first advanced seminar, and rapidly continued the theoretical development of her original practically related motivations. She passed her exams with distinction in far less time than normal.

And as is demonstrated here in exemplary fashion: the best propaedeutic is reality!

Little Red Riding Hood
in Church History

The period in which the events occurred that became known as the "Red Riding Hood Turmoil" is familiar to Church historians. It all happened at the end of the fifteenth century, in the time we call the "eve" of the Western Reformation. The work of Bernhold Read (whose research on Martin Luther has led students to give him the pet name "Read-Luther") has brought this final epoch of the Middle Ages into the light of historical knowledge from the point of view both of general history and of the history of theology. In addition, Henneke Güstrow and Matthäus Pitcherhost have done pioneering work for understanding this era, the former through his cultural history and the latter through his economic and social-historical analysis.

Germany was still primarily a rural land at this time. Only five percent of the German population lived in cities, none of which had more than 50,000 inhabitants. Germany (to the extent that the historian would not consider as anachronistic this term belonging to the period of the nation-states) was thus one giant contiguous forest region except where the forest had been cleared to make the land arable, but this was done to a far lesser extent than we tend to imagine today. The problem of criminality was proportionally less, and thus it could certainly happen that an older woman would live alone in a house in the forest, for which the infrastructure was limited to one solitary footpath through the forest. Of course there are certain indications that this situation changed in the wake of the Red Riding Hood Turmoil.

And now to the leading figure: Little Red Riding Hood was the daughter of parents of modest property, belonging to the emerging middle class. Their property, indeed, dwindled in the course of their lives due to economic decline, so that the parents fell into poverty in their old age. They were artisans, and hence entirely bound to the system of regulations of their class and guild, including both its protective aspects and its restrictions, so that they were not used to autonomous thinking and action. Therefore it was understandable that they clothed their daughter with the headdress of their guild, a red hood. Scholars still dispute whether the red hood signifies the textile worker or the dyer, but we can bracket this question for the moment. We also know that a great number of names originate from this period that are still in use in only slightly modified form today, and that these names identify their bearers either according to profession, locale, or some other particular characteristic.

For example, the name "Pesch" stems from the word "Pesche" (spoken with a long *e*!) and this in turn from the Latin *pascua*. One can therefore conclude that the bearers of this name (which incidentally is the name of a place on the lower Rhine), at one time possessed meadows and therefore pastured livestock. Thus for the church historian familiar with the state of research it is in no way out of the ordinary that a girl at that time was called "Little Red Riding Hood." The name designates the bearer simply according to what she wore on her head.

At the same time, the exact cause that produced the Red Riding Hood Turmoil is for the most part lost in the dark recesses of the past. Light can perhaps best be shed on the event through a comparison with the watershed of Luther's Reformation. Such a comparison is completely legitimate. For the people of that age, having grown heartily tired of late-scholastic hair-splitting, were in search of a fresh, new theological approach, and some even believed themselves to have found one. Such sayings as "I feel as if I am born again," later employed by Luther to designate the new insight he experienced, were quite common at the time. Luther thus stands in this distinguished linguistic tradition, and one cannot even exclude the possibility that he was aware of the Red Riding Hood Turmoil, although, as will be demonstrated, it probably took place hundreds of miles from his home.

Whatever the case may be, it is known that the parents of Little Red Riding Hood, along with countless fellow believers in the sermon-loving late Middle Ages, regularly went to hear preaching on Sunday afternoon. On a certain autumn Sunday —it is disputed whether the year was 1482 or 1483—they heard a sermon on Matt 25:31-46, Jesus' great discourse on the last judgment. They were "broken asunder," one might say, as once did Luther in referring to his own insight. From then on they spoke no more of their original intention to send their youngest daughter to a nunnery, as was the custom of the time. The parents understood anew that the nature of Christian existence no longer consisted in flight from the world, but instead in the praxis of neighborly love grounded in faith. All theories were secondary to this, or to be more precise: orthopraxis must condition and precede orthodoxy both structurally and intrinsically. In short, one would not be going too far in seeing here a distant precursor to a present theological trend that is known by the name of "political theology." So the parents packed baked goods and wine in a basket, gave it to their daughter, and sent her into the forest to bring these gifts to her grandmother who lived there; in doing so she would execute a praxis-oriented deed of neighborly love. Incidentally, no one has succeeded up to the present moment in determining whether it was the maternal or paternal grandmother.

The minor details about "baked goods" and "wine" reveal much to historians, but they will not immediately give way to pious associations and see here an allusion to the celebration of the Lord's Supper. Instead, with the down-to-earth realism characteristic of historians, they will draw conclusions about the location of the events. Why not oatmeal and beer, or rice and tea? Baked goods and wine indicate on the one hand a location that must be cold (for reasons soon to be discussed), but on the other hand must be near a wine-growing region. Third, as the *combination* of baked goods and wine reveals, this location must be subject to French influence. In short, the place must be in the Western Rhineland, in the mountain massif. (One thinks of the Eifel, the Hunsrück, or the Pfälzerwald.)

More southerly regions are ruled out because they either lack wolves (wolves are not commonly found in warmer regions), or, as for example in the Alps, no wine grows there. At any rate wolves must have been quite numerous in the forests of this region, and that is no marvel when one considers that the last wolf was shot on German soil around 1850 in the Bavarian forest.

Hence it is not surprising that a wolf would cross paths with a girl in the forest. The wolf always carried a negative connotation in the Christian-Biblical tradition of course, but this apparently had not yet made a strong impression in the general consciousness of believers before the Red Riding Hood Turmoil. It was no wonder that Little Red Riding Hood at first approached the wolf without trepidation. The wolf on the other hand shamelessly and ruthlessly exploited two cultural and historical factors that are not easily conceivable today: the inadequate infrastructure (the fact that only one path led safely to the destination), and a natural environment completely untouched and not damaged by any ecological contamination. So it was easy for him to point out to Little Red Riding Hood the abundance of pretty flowers, which she might make into a bouquet and bring to her grandmother, and then to slip away stealthily, in the certain knowledge that Little Red Riding Hood would need a significant amount of time before she found her way back to the one secure path through the virgin forest.

What followed we only know from the accounts and the perspective of those concerned, since there are naturally no witnesses. The historian will therefore approach the reports handed down and especially the dialogues with the required methodological caution, and will be reticent in judging the intensive efforts at interpretation by the colleague in systematic theology at this very point (see above, "Little Red Riding Hood: A Systematic Theology"), being mindful of the problem that we do not have a secure line of tradition for the *ipsissima vox* (the authentic voice) of Little Red Riding Hood, or of the wolf, or of the grandmother. The *brutum factum* (brute fact), however, is indisputable: the wolf devoured the easily outwitted grandmother first, then the unsuspecting Little Red Riding Hood, and then (no surprise!) fell into a deep sleep.

The historian is on safe ground again when the hunter appears, for he is attested not only by witnesses, but by the outcome of the story and its subsequent effects. The "hunter"—at that time an occupation not yet alienated into that of a "forest warden"—*lived* from the hunt, and did not perform his task as a leisure sport. Thus he knew how to interpret the smallest sign in the forest and on the forest floor, and he discovered the indisposed wolf. The result is well known.

The news of this naturally traveled far and wide, much as did Luther's Theses. Soon fairy tales, sagas, poems, and songs were composed about "Little Red Riding Hood." This upside of the Red Riding Hood Turmoil of course had its downside: the systematic eradication of the wolf from Europe can be shown to have begun at the end of the fifteenth century—to the point that the wolf would have to be artificially reintroduced into Germany in wildlife parks such as the National Park in the Bavarian forest.

The church historian, to the degree that this field is a theological one, can avoid only with difficulty the fact that the Red Riding Hood Turmoil is a historical paradigm for the animosity between humans and animals, which is a consequence of sin. All the more will historians be able, from the perspective of their discipline, to help in shedding light on the eschatological prophecy of Isaiah: "The wolf shall live with the lamb . . . and the lion shall eat straw like the ox" (Isa 11:6-7).

Little Red Riding Hood:
An Old Testament Perspective

Among the stories drawn from the Old Testament, the midrash of Little Red Riding Hood is exceptionally well known, even among those of our contemporaries who otherwise have not read a line of the Bible, certainly not the Old Testament. There are two explanations: first, the story's thematic treatment of the fundamental and universal human condition: life, acting according to the divine command, the threat of death, and unexpected salvation. The second stems from the parallels that (for that very reason) this biblical story has in the treasury of fables in many extra-biblical cultures, even those, for example the Germanic culture, that have not been affected by the world of the Old Testament.

1. *The State of Research*

For a long time scholarship took for granted that the story was *only* a midrash, in other words a freely formed pedagogical narrative whose purpose is to clarify a theological truth: in this case a tale with prophetic content and eschatological import. More recent research, however, has shown that the narrative in all probability rests on an etiological legend. Just as Genesis 3, among other things, attempts to explain the "cause" (*aitīa*) of the unusual revulsion humanity has toward snakes, likewise the story of Little Red Riding Hood elucidated the cause of the particular hostility between humans and wolves. This hostility demands a special clarification, since it is known that the wolf by nature does not feed on humans, but only on sick and dying animals.

At the forefront of the latest line of research is the biblical archaeology of Edward Northern, who has found scarabs in the territory east of the Jordan, a former forest region. These finds give indication of a historical kernel in the Little Red Riding Hood story.[1] According to the images on the underside of the scarabs there must have been at one time a plague of wolves in that region that resulted in the loss of many human lives, but that ended as suddenly as it had begun (so one can conclude from the fossil bones of wolves that can be dated with precision). The scarabs display images that show how the plague of wolves came to an end through a miraculous intervention of God. In addition, scholars have found hieroglyphics on scarabs, and after a long and arduous process of piecing together a translation of the text, have found that the meaning of the hieroglyphics displays an amazing similarity to Gen 3:15. A divine decree is given to the wolf: "I will put enmity between you and the shepherd. You shall lie in wait for him, and he shall split open your belly."

From this inscription we can understand how an etiological legend quickly arose, which can be reconstructed as a literary source of the Little Red Riding Hood tale. Of course the story gained its historical efficacy first in the form of the biblical midrash. Hence the researches of Niklas Köchel and Bertold Najowski remain unsurpassed to date. These two have given an airtight explanation of the prophetic (classification: "cause-effect relationship") and the historical background in Eastern religion (classification: "assistance on the following day"). For this reason the collection of relevant contributions by Niklas Köchel is respectfully dubbed by scholars the "Köchel Catalogue."

2. The Content of the Tale

Now we come to the biblical-theological content of this instructional narrative. First let us recapitulate the original text.

1. A scarab is a piece of jewelry in the form of a dung beetle, with decorations or characters on the flat underside, especially common in ancient Egypt, but also found as an import or imitation in Palestine and Syria. Note: this footnote is not a fairy tale.

Unfortunately, in the course of the Lutheran decisions on the content of the Old Testament canon, the text found no place in the Luther Bible (for this matter see the well-known and insightful essay by our colleague Bernhold Read!). Instead one finds this story among the pseudepigraphical *k^etubim* (writings) in the Wisdom literature in a Catholic Bible.

A young girl, who bore the name "Little Red Riding Hood" (v. 1: more on this later), is sent by her parents to "the other side of the forest" where her grandmother lived, to bring her freshly baked bread and wine (v. 2). On the way she has an encounter with a lone wolf, who on this particular day was apparently looking in vain for prey, and (here the saga can no longer be distinguished from history) enters into a conversation with him (vv. 3-4). Little Red Riding Hood lets herself be distracted, and collects a few bitter herbs for her grandmother (v. 5), when the wolf suddenly disappears (v. 6). Little Red Riding Hood arrives at her grandmother's house (v. 7), where the wolf has already gained entrance with wolf-like cunning, devoured the grandmother, and, putting on her clothes, laid himself on her shabby bed (vv. 8-9). Little Red Riding Hood does not recognize the wolf, and allows herself once again to be drawn into conversation with him—until the wolf is overcome with greed and devours Little Red Riding Hood as well (vv. 10-14). That this story nevertheless has a happy ending is owing to the circumstance that this isolated region is also the preferred location of shepherds and their flocks, and Palestinian shepherds are thoroughly familiar with wolves (vv. 15-16). A shepherd, intending to bring the grandmother a fresh cut of lamb (v. 17), discovers the indisposed wolf, kills it, cuts open its stomach, and rescues Little Red Riding Hood and her grandmother at the last minute (vv. 18-19). The account concludes with a great feast with roasted lamb, bitter herbs, bread, and wine (vv. 20-22).

3. Historical-Critical Exegesis

Verse 1: The name "Little Red Riding Hood," familiar to us in modern translations, undoubtedly represents an anticipatory "hermeneutical appropriation" of a different culture. In Palestine and neighboring regions the women wear veils, not hoods. In the original Hebrew text we find one of the familiar *status-constructus* formulations on the model: "the statue of my silver" = "my silver statue." In this case the text reads literally: "the veil of my red." Grammatically both translations are possible: "my red veil" and "the veil of my redness" in the sense of "for my red hair." Although Hebrew has the adjective "red" (*?edom*), which renders a *status-constructus* formulation superfluous, and although redheads were found in the region—one need only think of the Edomites—the first translation has been accepted by scholars. Therefore I will use the translation "Red Veil" in the rest of the essay.

Verse 2: The isolated living situation of the grandmother— "on the far side of the forest" must refer to the Jordan Valley, which, as we know, in ancient times was located beyond the forest's edge—is astonishing. Moreover, this isolation is even more extraordinary in the context of the traditional extended family. Her isolated life can only be explained as the result of a forced banishment, probably due to a skin disease, and every ancient historian knows how baffled Near Eastern society was by skin diseases, for medical and therefore also for religious reasons. Thus when Red Veil is sent by her parents to her banished grandmother with basic foodstuffs we can draw only one conclusion: both the parents and the daughter are deeply convinced that banishment from one's fellow human beings is against the will of God. Her visit is a prophetic action. We have before us an early witness, much earlier than that of Israel's writing prophets, to a fundamental aspect of the prophetic tradition, possibly even the source of that tradition, heretofore neglected by scholars.

Verses 3-4: As we have already noted, the fossil records leave no doubt about the credibility of the report of the wolf's appearance. Of course, zoologists inform both Orientalists and Old Testament scholars that the fossil findings could possibly be from hyenas. They may represent the remains of an evolutionary variant of the species we find today in the park on the Lüneberg Heath or in the Bavarian forest park. The possibilities of historical certainty are of course absent as regards the "conversation" between Red Veil and the wolf—no differently than in regard to the historical kernel of Jesus' miracles. We can only say that *some kind* of at least non-verbal communication must have taken place, because otherwise the rest of the story is incomprehensible.

Verse 5: It is difficult to explain why Red Veil and her parents did not think of the bitter herbs *earlier,* if they were in fact necessary. In light of the outcome of the story (see vv. 20-22) the herbs must have a providential significance that can only be fully developed in a concluding theological interpretation.

Verses 6-7: When we consider that the forest received an abundant amount of rain at that time (more than 500 mm. per year), and thus had the character of a subtropical rain forest, the unnoticed disappearance of the wolf should not surprise us. Nevertheless, primitive children like Red Veil can find their way through the rainforest despite the lack of infrastructure.

Verses 7-9: The fate of the grandmother at the hands of the wolf does not require any commentary, since the textual account corresponds completely to the adaptations in other cultural settings, for example the German tale of Little Red Riding Hood.

Verses 10-14: The content of these verses is also common to the parallels in the non-Hebraic store of fairy tales. However, the Old Testament scholar must ask herself or himself how, given the degree of prophetic consciousness that one must acknowledge on the part of Red Veil and her parents, Red Veil could have remained so unsuspecting of the wolf a second time. Despite reservations about premature systemization, the biblical scholar cannot here suppress a recollection of the phrase associated with a colleague in the field of systematic theology, Paul Tillich: "dreamlike innocence."

Verses 15-19: With vv. 15-16 the Orientalist is again on secure ground. It is obvious that one cannot talk about a "hunter" here, given the cultural situation. On the contrary, the reliability of the historical kernel is demonstrated by the fact that a *shepherd* appears, and that he intends to bring a lamb to the grandmother. At that time the shepherds were outcasts as well, the epitome of the scorned and marginalized, as of course we hear every year in the Christmas readings. The marginalized practice solidarity toward one another—that is the simple con-clusion we must draw from this story. We also know about the hereditary enmity between shepherds and wolves from John 10:1-21. Thus it is no surprise that the shepherd here reacts im-mediately. "*One* wolf less," the shepherd must have thought to himself. Thank God he cut carefully—we may certainly sup-pose that Red Veil and the grandmother made signs from the wolf's belly advising him to use caution.

Verses 20-22: Now the historical findings also show Red Veil's search for bitter herbs to have been providential. Without explicitly intending it, Red Veil had brought the garnish for a lamb roast that was not originally foreseen. After her great ex-perience of liberation, however, it is clear that the minimal pro-vision of basic foodstuffs must yield to a great feast, replete with roast lamb, bitter herbs, bread, and wine. What person fa-miliar with the Scriptures would not be reminded of the Pass-over meal? The scholar cannot avoid certain conclusions. The previously mentioned wolf findings are dated to the nine-teenth century B.C.E., that is, before the Israelite settlement, and that settlement is connected with the tradition of the Passover meal preceding the Exodus from the "land of Egypt . . . the house of slavery" (Deut 5:6). The conclusion is undeniable: the Passover tradition finds its roots in the Red Veil midrash. And insofar as the Christian eucharistic celebration is related to the Passover meal (although this is questioned), it too stems from the Red Veil midrash.

4. Theological Interpretation

All detailed historical-critical explanation is only a supple-mentary aid to interpretation, and is sometimes almost a lux-ury for students of theology! What would become of us if we had to wait for the work of such scholars as Northern, Köchel and Najowski, for example, before we could adequately understand the biblical story of Red Veil and translate it into Christian practice! We say "no thank you" to a professors' Church, even one introduced by such surreptitious means! What binds us and obligates us in obedience to the word of

God is the *text*, in its current canonical (or deuterocanonical) form—not etiological saga, and certainly not the fundamental *brutum factum*, but instead the midrash in its final redacted form. Or to state it in the specialized terminology of biblical scholarship, our hermeneutical duty lies not with the diachronic, but the synchronic reading of the text.

From the exegesis of the parables of Jesus we know that one must pay attention always and only to the *tertium comparationis*, the mediating element between the tale and its meaning, in a *parable. Midrash,* on the other hand, is more closely related to *allegory* in that *all* details have a theological meaning. And above all else, the actors and their actions are not to be understood individually, but collectively. Adam and Eve are not a prehistoric couple—we are all Adam and Eve. Red Veil, her parents, the grandmother, the shepherd, the wolf: who are *they?*

We must begin with the figure of the grandmother. As the historical-critical exegesis disclosed, the grandmother represents the outcasts, the marginalized, and the scorned. The rest are those who are in some way related to the outcasts, and more or less clearly place themselves in the course of the "cause and effect connection" on the side of the outcasts. If we carefully consider every hermeneutical step from then to now, and render the ancient text literally "apt" today, thus effectively bringing the *krisis* to speech, then there can be no doubt in the end: the grandmother represents the undergraduates. They are the outcasts of the university; nobody will dispute that life in the university is more pleasant and runs more smoothly to the extent that the undergraduates remain outsiders. That these outcasts are represented by a grandmother, not only a woman, but an old woman, of course belongs to the illustrative aspect (the "Bildhälfte") of the story and must be transcended as a result of the new hermeneutical situation.

One can interpret Red Veil as the group of graduate assistants and lecturers who transport the basic intellectual nourishment to the outcasts. As a sub-human being, the wolf represents all the anonymous powers that exclude the students and block their path to the intellectual nourishment: rigid requirements, lack of classroom space, curtailed library hours, government cutbacks, and much more. Obviously the parents are the professors. That the story concerns wife *and* husband is again part of the illustrative aspect, since as we know, despite all the progress made by women, there are still practically no women professors. The modern outcasts are unfortunately also scholarly half-orphans. It is not a little noteworthy that the parents in the midrash (that is, the professors in reality) are fully in agreement with the prophetic protest of Red Veil (the assistants and lecturers), but do not themselves go to the outcasts. Instead they let their ministering angels deal with them.

The interpretation of the shepherd appears the most difficult. But when we liberate ourselves from an old, narrow, bourgeois view it is not *so* difficult: the shepherd who rescues the situation and provides the feast is the bishop (male or female). For even bishops can belong to the outcasts, as one sees in other, non-German and European regions of the world.

All of these factors then come together, and the kerygma, yes, the *gospel* of this midrash can be summed up in one sentence: "I desire steadfast love and not sacrifice" (Hos 6:6).

It is also noteworthy in light of this kerygma that the parents are not present at the celebration of liberation. But the professors are quite rightly excluded from a celebration of the experience of mercy. For when has anyone ever heard that professors had anything to do with liberation or mercy?

Little Red Riding Hood:
A Missiological Perspective

As the latest scholarship in missiology demonstrates, the Little Red Riding Hood parable had its roots and probably a historical core as well in events that took place in the seventeenth century (according to the Christian calendar), in the upper reaches of the Indian subcontinent, a region heavily influenced by Buddhism. The extensive research of Buddhism expert Olaf Seeland has concluded that "Riding Hood" is a Europeanization, and probably the color "red" is a typical case of Eurocentric imperialism. The girl most assuredly wore the headdress of the poor: a wide, flat straw hat. The tradition of a color can probably be traced to the floral decoration. Accordingly one must re-translate "Little Red Riding Hood" as "Straw Flower," and we will henceforth do so. The story yields an early example of interreligious encounter and the intercultural transmission of Christianity. Unfortunately it set no precedent, probably due to the so-called "rites controversy" that soon followed in neighboring China, which set the Christian missions in Asia back for centuries, and not only those of the Catholic Church, which had picked the quarrel in the first place.

The parents of Straw Flower had recently converted to Christianity. As is often the case with converts, they took separation from their non-Christian environment quite seriously. Owing to circumstances, however, Straw Flower attended a Buddhist school, and grew up "religiously bilingual," as one might say. This fact, and her deep conviction about the ineffable namelessness of God, led to her lasting absorption with questions of interreligious dialogue. Her parents did not fail to notice this development, and they sought frantically to divert her from such views. Therefore they arranged for Straw Flower to undertake what they thought would be a defining Christian task, a concrete expression of the absoluteness and exclusivity of the Christian claim: an act of neighborly love. Straw Flower was to cross the mountains terraced with rice fields to bring rice cakes and sake (rice wine) to her grandmother, who lived alone on the other side. Straw Flower accepted the task with delight: for one thing, Christianity in no way undermined the Asiatic tradition of the patriarchal family, entailing the unconditional obedience of the children, especially the girls; on the contrary, Christianity had immediately "baptized" these traditions. In addition, Straw Flower was a believing Christian. But she was happy to perform the task above all else because, although her parents did not realize this, she saw in it a path into the "great abyss" and to the "true light." Thus she hoped to experience the possibility of joining the Buddhist and Christian concepts of the person in her very self.

Straw Flower set out. We should by no means imagine that a seventeenth-century path through the Indian hinterland remotely resembles a German hiking route through the Black Forest. It is no wonder that she got lost. Paradoxically, a Bengal Tiger (the "wolf" is, once again, a Eurocentric redaction) helped Straw Flower to regain her orientation. There had to be water where he was going, and only there can the grandmother have resided.

As one can say, in the words of the well-known title of a book by Reginald and Michaela McBridges, the Buddhist idea of universal oneness perceives the world as a "universe full of grace." With such a mindset, Straw Flower approached the tiger without fear—perhaps, though the sources are silent on this point, she suppressed her fear. The dialogue between Straw Flower and the tiger may actually have taken place in a completely real sense, though such a thing is unimaginable to us intellectualized Europeans.

Straw Flower's grandmother remained a Buddhist, and therefore Straw Flower knew that she was of course imbued with the truth of the unity of all things, and believed that natural herbs could alleviate the pains of old age. (A side note: even in Europe, flowers were originally given as healing herbs, not room decorations.) At any rate, Straw Flower gathered the herbs, keeping an eye on the direction in which the tiger trotted off, and later followed his tracks. Thus she found her grandmother's house. There, in the mean time, had occurred an event that after all furnished an argument for the accuracy of the Christian notion of the shattered relationship between people and animals brought on by the Fall, a total disruption as regards humanity, and therefore independent of any individual religious conviction. In the spirit of her holistic religiosity the grandmother sought uninhibited and loving acquaintance with the tiger. She had certainly spoken warmly to him and petted him, as she did with her granddaughter. The tiger misinterpreted this as aggression and acted "holistically" from his perspective: he devoured the grandmother wholly. Then he lay down in the grandmother's bed. This was not a twentieth-century European bed; rather, it was a straw bed adorned with flowers, a bed that the tiger no doubt confused with his own bed in the wild.

In line with her interreligious interests, Straw Flower had practiced meditation at home with the hope of enriching and expanding her Christian spirituality. (A side note: the most recent publications of Theodosius Cobbs also refer frequently to this phenomenon. Its significance can scarcely be underestimated, for it paradigmatically anticipates encounter and efforts at dialogue such as those initiated in the work of the Jesuit Hugo Enomyia-Lassalle.) In the course of these exercises, then, Straw Flower had already transcended the stage of sitting meditation, and was now able to practice walking meditation. Thus one understands how she almost mechanically followed the tracks of the tiger while remaining deep in her meditation.

While still engaged in this effort to empty herself, Straw Flower reached her grandmother's hut and, in its dim light, failed to perceive that the tiger, instead of her grandmother, was lying on the bed. As regards the consequences of this confusion the European version of Little Red Riding Hood agrees entirely with the Asiatic account. Mistaking the tiger for her grandmother, Straw Flower inquired about the grandmother's eyes, ears, hands, and teeth, because she knew that her grandmother had certain pains of old age in these organs, which is no surprise considering the medical care at the time. Once again the tiger interpreted this as aggression, and what had happened with the grandmother was repeated. This was a real and enduring shock for Straw Flower, especially considering the peaceful, holistic encounter with the tiger on the path.

The rest of the story provides another demonstration of the plausibility of the Christian faith. One is tempted to recall the old truth of the *anima naturaliter christiana,* the "naturally Christian soul." By coincidence, a rice farmer came to the grandmother's hut to talk with her, as was his custom, and to take the opportunity to replenish her rice supply. In spite of his holistic perception of life, the rice farmer was no longer so convinced of the paradisiacal community shared between humans and animals, and in this realization he was conscious of the world's radical need for salvation. In a word, he was not far from the reign of God (see Mark 12:34). Not at all lost in meditation, he recognized the situation at once, strangled the tiger with his own hands (there is an especially potent aperitif produced in Asia that is supposed to provide the strength necessary for such things!), and liberated Straw Flower and her grandmother. Anyone familiar with Asia can imagine the feast that followed.

This experience had a profound effect on Straw Flower. She realized the uniqueness and once-and-for-all finality of death and resurrection in Christian terms. She no longer assented to notions of reincarnation, which are always associated with a self-redemptive mentality. Her efforts at interreligious exchange became more down to earth and lost every trace of syncretic tendency. From then on, her limitless openness to the transcendental reality of God and the divine mystery of the world as creation were united to an unconditional decision for the *eph' hapax,* the "once and for all" of the Christ event—a paradigm that even today points to the future.

Nevertheless, the European version of the story in the fairy tale of Little Red Riding Hood is an example of successful intercultural mediation between Buddhist and Christian thought —in this case an intercultural mediation in favor of *Buddhism!* For whether it detracts from the Christian claim to absoluteness or not, Little Red Riding Hood is Straw Flower!

Little Red Riding Hood:
A Practical Theology

Little Red Riding Hood never actually lived, of course. All the hypotheses of the Church historians, Old Testament scholars, and missiologists (see the preceding chapters) do rest on professionally appropriate courses of proof in each case, but they do not stand up to the obvious. It can now be demonstrated that the story of Red Riding Hood was invented in the 1950s by Jolly Short, the old master of (Lutheran) practical theology, as a so-called pastoral (and at the same time ecclesiotheoretical) model, in order to spell out both his theory of the Church and his concept of an appropriate contemporary pastoral praxis. Short thus became the inventor of "narrative theology" for the field of practical theology (henceforth abbreviated as PT, although at the risk of its being misunderstood as an advertisement for a certain journal in the field). This occurred a full decade before certain Protestant and Catholic systematic theologians acquired a taste for narrative theology! At the same time Short inaugurated a discussion in which nothing less was at stake than the plausibility and acceptability of the field of PT itself—one can in fact say without exaggeration: in which the scholarly and theoretical-practical socialization of PT into the theological community of scholars is at stake. We shall see this in detail when we give a meta-practical analysis of the story.

Little Red Riding Hood—named after a modish accessory of the 1950s—was a girl in the midst of an adolescent crisis: no longer a child, but not yet a self-sufficient adult. At this age one can expect certain narcissistic tendencies. Far too often these adolescent characteristics are exacerbated by irrational and insensitive religious instruction and preparation for Confirmation. This is not surprising, since the latest insights of PT, especially in the fields of religious pedagogy and pastoral care, as seen in the pioneering work of Wolf-Volkhart Oakes and Fulbert Redhill, could not have circulated among the older, overworked parish clergy.

Thus Little Red Riding Hood "enjoyed" a religious education that had not yet been stripped of ideology, one framed in the traditional style of "Christian instruction" in which, contrary to all the insights of developmental psychology (one need only think of the already proverbial five stages of religious development outlined by James Fowler), the legalism of confessional constraint represses the emergence of youthful self-esteem.

An "exodus" was necessary if Little Red Riding Hood were to overcome her adolescent crisis and arrive at the true "freedom of a Christian" in Luther's sense. Perceptive teachers and pastors with a broader educational background than can be expected of parish clergy, that is, pastors in the mold of a Paul Corneeling, would advise her to engage in a theme-centered interaction, symbolized in the word "exodus."

At this point the other intention of Short's model tale comes into play: the conception of an entirely new ecclesial theory. Experiences in our own time suggest that Christianity, at least in the form of the traditional Church, is a religion for the country population, a religious practice for agricultural societies. The numbers support this claim: in the country there is high participation in church life, while in the cities participation is low and declining. Thus there are already positions in the field of "urban ecclesiology" in theology departments. That the very opposite is historically true—that is, that Christianity first gained popularity in the urban areas—is not of interest to PT at the moment. However, it is dangerous in the long term to move pastors who are useless in the cities to the back of beyond, where it is thought they can't ruin anything. N.b.: I am not talking about *women* pastors, since there are none of those who would be useless in the city.

Thus Little Red Riding Hood is a model for a visionary pastoral strategy, according to which the Church must concern itself with the so-called "boondocks," which are threatened with neo-paganism, and of which there are plenty in northern Germany. Let us proceed to the story.

Little Red Riding Hood underwent what is called a "rite of passage" or "threshold rite," which is simultaneously a departure (from childhood) and an initiation (into the world of responsible adulthood). The rite is a sign of a breakthrough into a new life context—biblically an "exodus." Supported by a wise religious pedagogy on the part of her parents (who may have heard an enlightened sermon on 'the idea of Exodus' by the Old Testament scholar Edward Northern), Little Red Riding Hood clearly saw that she must leave the city for the country. As luck would have it, there was a person to whom she could direct her thematically-centered interaction, namely her grandmother, living in a solitary house in the forest, akin to those houses still standing in Dithmarsch in Schleswig-Holstein. The simultaneously ecclesio-theoretical and religio-pedagogical exercise required Little Red Riding Hood to bring her grandmother cake of her own baking—of course made with organic ingredients—and lilac-berry wine. (In Northern Germany wine made from grapes would make greater demands on the usual customs of the so-called "social market economy" than was theologically and prophetically sustainable.)

On the way to her grandmother's, Little Red Riding Hood encountered the wolf. It can easily be established by depth psychology that the wolf is the symbol of tradition, equipped with claws and teeth to suppress freedom, and placing obstacles to every mechanism for coping with the adolescent crisis. The wolf succeeds in delaying Little Red Riding Hood and causing her to interrupt her exodus by tempting her to pick flowers.

Northern Germans are amazed by this, for they do not know what a flower-studded meadow and a blooming forest look like. But the story transcends both time and geographical location. At any rate, the symbolism is clear: The flowers of tradition always have an advantage when it comes to temptation.

The grandmother also succumbs to the overwhelming power of tradition. There is no other way to interpret the symbol of the grandmother being devoured by the wolf. The same is the case with Little Red Riding Hood, who arrived shortly thereafter. Seduced by the flowers, she fell victim not only to the naked power of tradition, but also in part to her own youthful susceptibility. In the end, the legalism of the tradition did not triumph, thanks to those events that not without reason may stand under the title: *Dei providentia et ignorantia hominum*—roughly translated "through God's providence and in spite of human stupidity." The victory of tradition appears inevitable. But "coincidentally" a hunter appears, symbolizing PT as critical reflection on the actions of the Church, and therefore always on the edge of exclusion from Church and society. The hunter opens the way for Little Red Riding Hood, literally trapped by the tradition, to complete her exodus. Simultaneously he paradigmatically frees the grandmother, that is, the "boondocks," from the stranglehold of a traditional Church structure that suffocates living faith.

The story concludes with the "celebratory meal." Is it important to determine whether it was a "real" Lord's Supper? At any rate it is an expression of the enduring task of identifying all participants with the future power of the object of the Christian faith, with the transformation of tradition into new forms of being Church, and with the significance of PT for assisting ecclesial socialization: in short, for the unity of the missiological, ministerial, and pastoral Church.

Little Red Riding Hood:
A Perspective from Canon Law

Little Red Riding Hood was born into a mixed marriage, and, as one can only say with regret in the post-conciliar period, she was born in a period still subject to the marital law of the *Codex Iuris Canonici (CIC)* of 1917. She was thus involved in problems that would have been easier to resolve under the new *CIC* of 1983. For, as one must stress against intransigent theologians not accustomed to the way canon lawyers think, the new canon law is the faithful translation of the new directions in understanding the Church and its hierarchical structure introduced by the Second Vatican Council. At the same time, and this must be said as a prolegomenon, we are in no way criticizing the canon law, and especially the marital law, of the pre-conciliar period. In the legal realm it is the faithful champion of the existing official structure, and thus even in decisions subject to repeal it is truly "holy law," participating in the holy, incarnational essence of the Church, to which it gives a structure "precise as mathematics," as the famed Roman canonist from the Lateran University, Dino Stampa, has so unsurpassably articulated it.

With a heavy heart the Lutheran mother submitted to the regulation of canon 1061 *CIC* (unless otherwise noted, all references are to *CIC* 1917), and let her child be baptized in the Catholic Church. The Church is not unaware of the severity of such a demand, but the universality of its laws, which are the expression of the Church's self-understanding as the true Church of Jesus Christ, cannot be adjusted to individual need when this need contradicts the Church's self-understanding.

In any case, because of her baptism Little Red Riding Hood was subject to the provisions of canon 87, that is, she was *constituitur persona in ecclesia Christi*—"established as a person in the Church of Christ," a definition that Nicholas Moortown of happy memory so brilliantly interpreted in a number of studies. According to this provision she could fulfill all her duties in the Church and enjoy all her rights as long as a ban *(obex)* or a Church punishment *(censura)* did not prevent. Since the latter was not feasible due to her age (see canon 2226 in connection with canons 88, 89, and 2204), there only remained the possibility of a ban—of course without subjective guilt or responsibility.

But here is where Little Red Riding Hood's problems began, since the conduct of her confessionally-differing parents did not correspond to the requirements of canon law. For it happened, as it had to happen—and this is why in hindsight it still seems justified that the Church vigorously opposed confessionally mixed marriages for such a long time (see canon 1060): the mother had consented to a Catholic baptism, but the Catholic father, who was often away from home for business reasons, could not prevent the mother, who was under pressure from her Protestant parents, from breaking her promise by raising the child Lutheran and sending her to Lutheran religious instruction. Split church attendance soon became the norm, for the father strictly obeyed the regulations of canon 1258 §§ 1 and 2 in connection with canon 2316, which forbade any kind of common worship *(communicatio in sacris)* with a non-Catholic sect.

At the period when the well-known events took place that made Little Red Riding Hood the subject of every conversation, she could and should have already been to first confession and communion (see canon 854 § 4). Of course that was out of the question. On the contrary, it must have been as a demonstration of anti-Roman feelings that Little Red Riding Hood went into the forest to her grandmother at the very time when she should have been preparing for confession and first communion. From the Lutheran point of view her departure made a number of things clear: first, the fundamental Protestant critique of all the sacraments and of everything clerical and institutional; second, the principle of *"sola scriptura,"* which (allegedly) replaces the cultic with works of love of neighbor;

finally, the refutation of all Catholic accusations that Reformed theology does not place any value on the dictum that "pure faith" manifests itself in ethical behavior.

What, under the protection of and guided by the Church's maternal care, could have been a wonderful, child-like introduction to a life of faith, hope, and love according to God's commandments became under these circumstances a typically Protestant faith-exercise of the solitary individual. Little Red Riding Hood had to act "eye to eye with God," as Clemens Cardinal Ratzeburg concisely summarized Protestant spirituality many years ago. This could only result in placing excessive demands on the child, who required the spiritual guidance of an office that stands within the apostolic succession. This is evident from the child's helpless reliance on the wolf's whispers. Indeed, the canonist who is bound to the clarity of the juridical Church structure would not hesitate to say that one finds here an example of the systematic weakness of Protestant individualism. Often it is only a small step from the decision of a self-reliant individual supported by no institutional Church structure to the devolution into a diffuse nature religion—as some dubious developments in the present so-called "feminist theology" only too clearly show. Only a personalism that asserts without compromise the integrity of person over against nature helps against such a devolution, and it is in every case better preserved in the Catholic Church structure secured by a "holy law" than in a Protestant individualism that is only allegedly "personalist."

Let us return to the fate of Little Red Riding Hood. The wolf, who for this very reason must here be seen as a delegate of the "ruler of this world" (see John 14:30), succeeded in diverting the child from the clearly acknowledged instruction of divine law, namely the Fourth Commandment, and tempting her into following her own interests at the expense of the common good of the Church and society. N.b.: this transgression of divine law must be left to the clarification of the *forum internum* (see if necessary canon 258), since on the one hand Little Red Riding Hood was not yet a consenting adult and thus not capable of a criminal offense in the realm of canon law, and since on the other hand in the nature of things the lapse was not an act of disobedience against a Church superior, and therefore we do not need to take into account canon 89 in connection with canons 119 and 2214 § 1.

As the Church has always taught, the real punishment for sin consists in the effects naturally resulting from the act itself, and not in any externally imposed sentence. The ecclesiastical law of punishments, although a right essentially belonging to the Church (see canon 2214 § 1), has, in contrast, a predominantly medicinal character (see ibid., § 2). Hence Little Red Riding Hood's fate at the hands of the wolf clothed as Grandmother was in the first place the immanent punishment for her transgression of divine law, and there was no need for a punishment automatically imposed *(excommunicatio latae sententiae)* in accordance with canon 2217 § 1, 2°.

Nevertheless, following the example of her Lord, Holy Mother Church is inexhaustibly merciful even in her law of punishments. In this case the Church acted through the service of a high-ranking prelate and canon from Little Red Riding Hood's diocese. Through a papal indult dispensing from canon 138 this prelate was allowed to hunt in that area, where his family had certain hereditary tenant rights. As he was carrying out his familial duties on this day, he immediately recognized the situation in the grandmother's house. In particular he realized the true nature of the wolf, and accordingly performed an exorcism (driving out the devil) according to canons 1151 and 1152. He had abiding authority to do so from the local bishop. The wolf had to give back Little Red Riding Hood and the grandmother, and return to the one who sent him.

Even though the Church proved herself worthy of reliance here, in the sense of the First Vatican Council, in her "inexhaustible fertility in all good works" (Denzinger-Schönmetzer 3013), on the other hand it is no surprise that Little Red Riding Hood and her grandmother, in accord with Protestant understanding, attributed their salvation from death solely to God's undeserved mercy. They celebrated with a worship service of thanksgiving and a feast following the service, an action of which even the apostolic chair does not in any way disapprove. This means, at the same time, that even after her rescue through the aid of the ecclesiastical dignitary Little Red Riding

Hood still did not see any reason to return to the bosom of the Church in which she was baptized. This had consequences that were not foreseeable at the time of the events, but later, when the memory of the thing was revived, initiated heated discussions in the media.

For when she was old enough to marry, Little Red Riding Hood considered betrothal. Naturally she wanted a young Lutheran man. This deeply disturbed the conscience of her (as we recall) Catholic father. With good intentions, but poor planning, the father wanted by all means to prevent Little Red Riding Hood from entering a sacramentally invalid marriage. He made it clear to his future Lutheran son-in-law that their marriage would only be sacramentally valid if the son-in-law allowed a ceremony according to the Catholic rite, performed by a priest before two witnesses (according to canons 1094–1103). The future son-in-law was astonished. He asked why his pending marriage to the father's Lutheran daughter would not be valid, since the Church normally recognized the validity of marriages between baptized Protestant Christians according to canon 87 and canon 1036 § 1, and even, in accordance with its faith, viewed these marriages as sacramental. The father responded by explaining that on the basis of a 1949 decision by Pope Pius XII—in the interests of legal certainty—concerning canon 1099 § 2.2, baptism alone, and not one's religious or confessional upbringing, was decisive in this matter. In obedience to the canon law at the time, Little Red Riding Hood was baptized Catholic, and therefore a member of the Catholic Church. And the father did not forget to add, realistically, but in a quietly threatening tone, that in the case of a Protestant marriage it would always be possible for Little Red Riding Hood to abandon the marriage and marry another man, even a Catholic, since, from the perspective of canon law, no marriage would have taken place. The father also explained these facts to his daughter, not failing to add that if there was a Protestant ceremony her future "husband" could divorce her at any time and remarry in the Church, even marry a Catholic—of course only after obtaining the necessary papal dispensation, which, however, the local bishop regularly conferred within the parameters of the so-called quinquennial authority (the dispensational authority of the apostolic chair that is delegated to the bishops every five years).

Both of the betrothed were so rooted in their Lutheran faith that the demand to follow the provisions of Catholic canon law appeared unreasonable. On the other hand, the pair did not want to ignore the dangers to which the bride's father had alerted them. The information about the situation under canon law had sowed doubt in their hearts. The young man revoked his proposal and a few years later married another young woman. Little Red Riding Hood remained unmarried.

Reporters from the tabloids and moderators of talk shows heard news of these events and recalled the unforgotten story of Little Red Riding Hood's childhood. They aroused an unprecedented media onslaught against the Catholic Church, and accused the Church of violating human rights. These events gave the opportunity to the wise Pope Paul VI, the pre-precursor of the present pope, to review the existing marital laws on the one hand in light of possible abuses, and on the other hand in view of the pastoral consequences thereof. In 1970 the papal bull *Matrimonia mixta* ("Mixed Marriages") restructured Church law regarding mixed marriages. After taking care of some relatively simple dispensation formalities, couples from different faiths have their own choice of wedding ceremony: Catholic, Protestant, or if necessary even a state ceremony, in each case receiving full recognition from the Church. All the previous automatic excommunications that had been enacted were now revoked. The 1983 *CIC* incorporated the new regulations in canons 1124–1129, adding to them the determination that—contrary to Pius XII's rule—Catholics who have separated from the Church through a formal act are no longer subject to the Church's formal requirements (canon 1117 *CIC* 1983).

After 1970 the "Little Red Riding Hood Case" could never happen again. In the Jubilee Year of 2000 an international congress of canon lawyers in Rome is to evaluate how the new regulation of marital law (brought on indirectly by the "Little Red Riding Hood Case") has stood the test in the past thirty years, and whether these provisions will pave a new way for the Church at the beginning of the third millennium.

Little Red Riding Hood:
A New Testament Perspective

The story of Little Red Riding Hood—in order to avoid a technical argument relevant only to other scholars in the field we will not bother to question whether Little Red Riding Hood was her original name, and how it might have sounded in Aramaic (Jesus' native tongue); however, on this point see the relevant hypotheses of my Old Testament colleague!—at first glance, the story of Little Red Riding Hood reads like a parable. There is a clear story part, an equally clear application, unreal features in the story part that relate to the point of the tale (a talking wolf, two people whom the wolf can apparently swallow without harming, and who can be rescued again unharmed from his stomach); the story is told in a quite vivid manner free of any abstract concepts and, like Jesus' parables, it is accessible to a literary-critical analysis.

At second glance, however, a *form-critical* classification within the parable genre faces insurmountable difficulties. First of all, parables are not like allegories: not every feature of the story part corresponds to something outside the story. Instead there is only *one* so-called *tertium comparationis,* only *one* feature that can be carried over from the story part into the application and thus constitutes the "lesson" of the parable. In Little Red Riding Hood there are quite obviously a number of elements in the story part that contain a point, and therefore can be applied outside the story.

Second, both the literary form and the application lack the single major theme of the Jesus parables: the reign of God. The story of Little Red Riding Hood does *not* begin: "The kingdom of God is like a young girl named Little Red Riding Hood, who. . . ." Finally, implausible features are not reserved for parables alone. We also find them in the so-called "nature miracles," in regard to which neither an exegete nor a systematician can determine precisely what historical root lies concealed within the biblical narrative—one need only think of the coin for the Temple tax in the fish's mouth (Matt 17:27). This particular story in fact gives us a pointer: it is a sequence of questionable incidents with a clear moral application at the end. The case is somewhat similar with the stories of the good Samaritan (Luke 10:25-37) and the Pharisee and the toll collector (Luke 18:10-14). From a form-critical perspective this is an exemplary story in which the positive main character is to be imitated point for point. The moral quintessence is: whoever practices mercy is in the presence of God in grace and will be saved, even from situations that are one's own fault.

But at this point the *redaction-critical* complications begin. We owe the collection of "unknown sayings of Jesus," to which the story of Little Red Riding Hood belongs, to the meticulous scholarship of Joachim Isaias. His "grandson-student" Timothy Scratch has shown, however, that the story has not come down to us as it came from the lips of Jesus. Its original *Sitz im Leben* is the controversy with the scribes concerning the balancing of Law and mercy as ways to salvation, as we find it, for example, in Matt 9:10-13; 12:1-8. The version handed down to us has turned the original example story into a soteriological sermon whose kerygma clearly reveals a redactor influenced by Pauline theology: on the path through suffering and death, that is, on the way of the Cross, to resurrection! To this point nobody has determined whether the original story has its historical roots in Jesus or if the tale goes back to an independent Jewish narrative that Jesus reformulated (similarly to the parable of the great feast). Perhaps the old master in this area of research, Nicholas H. Hunsbrook, on the basis of his comprehensive expertise in Jewish sources from the time of Jesus, can shed light on this shadowy question in the near future.

Naturally the object of our interpretation must be the narrative we have received, that is, the version subsequent to *Paulinist redaction;* everything else would ultimately rest on tentative reconstructions. Hence the story as narrated runs as follows:

Little Red Riding Hood was the daughter of prosperous Jerusalem property-holders with vineyards in the fertile lowlands descending toward the Mediterranean. It was a given aspect of their faith that they would provide a grandmother living in those lowlands with the fundamental foodstuffs of that country, including bread and *vin ordinaire*. In doing this, they were following the prophetic praise of mercy, Jesus' starting point, and for the Pauline final redactor a reminder of Gal 5:6 and the Pauline paraenesis. For these parents there was not even a need for the Fourth Commandment. Instead, we could see behind their actions the full development of an idea that later appears in the letter to the Hebrews in the phrase "fathers and mothers in faith" (Hebrews 11).

Thus Little Red Riding Hood is sent off. On the way she encounters the wolf. For the form-critical problems, see above; as regards the application we will presently say what is necessary. The cunning animal succeeds in convincing Little Red Riding Hood that the gifts intended for her grandmother need supplementation for practical and theological reasons: human beings do not live by bread alone, but also from herbs and fruits. Little Red Riding Hood succumbs in good conscience to the alluring suggestion of a subtle "justification through works," of furtive performance-oriented thinking. She does not rely exclusively on the word of the promise, but instead "does the evil that she does not want" (see Rom 7:15, 19) and thus gives the wolf, unnoticed, an advantage over her grandmother. She, innocent and vulnerable like all who live by mercy instead of the Law, succumbs just like Little Red Riding Hood to the artful temptations of the wolf, to whom applies, and by no remote stretch, the saying from the Wisdom literature about "a wolf in sheep's clothing." She pays for her innocence with the awful, violent death of a righteous prophet, or so it appears. Little Red Riding Hood, her thoughts full of *kauchēsis*, boasting of her augmented gifts, arriving at her grandmother's house, is to be immediately destroyed along with them. Deeply absorbed in questioning the changed appearance of "Grandmother," and thus failing to recognize "inwardly" the "ravenous wolf" (see Matt 7:15), she again enters into conversation with the wolf, at the end of which the wolf, as is his wont, loses control and literally devours Little Red Riding Hood like an innocent lamb. Jesus' story here anticipates his later saying: "See, I am sending you out like sheep into the midst of wolves" (Matt 10:16).

The conclusion of the story clearly contains mythological elements that Jesus himself did not try to eliminate in his original version. They tell us that suffering and death for the sake of mercy signify a substitution or representation, through which new life is given to others. There is need only for someone who will put it into effect, here symbolized in the figure of the hunter. And this new life—how could it be otherwise in the case of a new life given by God—is a life of joy and peace, which one cannot conceive in a Jewish context without a feast.

In the history of research the work of Egbert Wild has earned him special prominence in the interpretation of this (as explained above) kerygmatic example story told by Jesus. On the lips of Jesus, as already indicated, the story is directed at those who put the letter of the Law above the situational duty to show mercy. It tells them: "Even the person who succumbs to demonic temptation in an act of mercy does not fall short of salvation." The kerygmatization of course removes limitations and universalizes the group-specific admonition. Little Red Riding Hood is a soteriological model demonstrating the human path toward God's salvation. To put it bluntly: *we are all Little Red Riding Hood.* We should recognize and understand ourselves in her. From this analysis we can recognize four intertwined motifs in this proclamatory narrative:

1. There is the motif of Christian *diakonia.* In the background is the Pauline paraenesis, especially Galatians 6. The indicative must become the imperative. Faith works through love, and whoever bears another's burden fulfills the law of Christ. The expression of this fundamental connection is the basket with bread and wine, symbols of life's necessities. And Red Riding Hood's subtle *parabasis,* her "offense," was to have falsified this symbol by supplementing it with things that are merely enjoyable. No, it is in concern for the *necessities of life* and for that alone that *koinonia,* solidary community with the grandmother, is concretely embodied.

2. The second motif concerns the wolf as a symbol for the satanic threat to human salvation. Solemn passages confirm

this meaning: Matt 7:15; 10:16; John 10:12; Acts 20:29. The wolf draws Little Red Riding Hood away from the right path and directs her attention away from what alone is necessary. This is a typical biblical and New Testament motif.

3. The third motif is the moment of "anti-salvation" history, expressed in the success of the wolf in radically calling into question Red Riding Hood's diaconal intention and thus the kerygmatic significance of her actions. Thus the story of Little Red Riding Hood is at the same time a summary of anti-salvation history. The human being refuses—with the best intentions, from his or her point of view—the divine commission and surrenders the field to God's adversary. It is the time of God's forbearance (see Rom 2:4; 3:26) that, within history, permits the adversary to forestall the accomplishment of God's intentions.

4. The fourth motif is that of the ultimate establishment of justice. The arrival of the hunter has a messianic significance; his actions overcome the disaster, and the agent of disaster is plunged into eternal death.

In the course of theological exegesis these kerygmatic motifs combine to yield an overall interpretation, an observation, and a message.

The Overall Interpretation: The story of Little Red Riding Hood is the soteriological model complementing that of the "Suffering Servant." Let me anticipate the obvious objection: If we reckon with genuine sayings of Jesus outside the canonical tradition at all, why must we exclude the possibility of further authentic soteriological interpretations in addition to those contained in the canonical texts? The complementarity consists in the fact that the "Suffering Servant" symbolizes the substitutional assumption of the debt by Jesus, representing, so to speak, the hamartiocentric dimension of the salvation event, while Little Red Riding Hood stands for the disclosure of new life in the solidarity of all—the rich with the poor, the healthy with the sick, the young with the old, women with men. There can be no doubt that these positive dimensions of the salvation event have not been given the proper attention throughout the history of Christianity, especially in a narrow Lutheran tradition, although Luther himself is not to blame. Thus there is indeed theological-historical tragedy in the fact that the necessary counteremphasis provided by the Little Red Riding Hood story, and most especially in its kerygmatic version, was unable, because of the contingencies of the construction of the canon, to develop an enduring influence.

The Observation: Once one ventures into such new territory of research one cannot help but notice that the story also makes a clear statement about the woman question. Unfortunately we cannot even hint at a more thorough treatment here; that remains for another reflection. We can say this: it is hardly a coincidence that the positive major characters are all women. The father remains entirely in the shadows. At most he harvested the grapes and pressed the wine. Without a doubt the mother baked the bread. In complete contrast to the spirit of the times the daughter was sent on the dangerous journey instead of a son, and in addition the purpose of the journey involved a woman. The hunter?—his function did not extend beyond that of assistance in service of life. More than anything, he mirrors the distant light of a past matriarchy, as seen in Gen 2:24, according to which the *man* leaves his own family to enter the family of the woman, not the other way around.

The insignificant role of the man is emphasized, finally, by the *message*. The conclusion of the story has a clearly mythological character. A modified version of Bultmann's famous dictum applies here as well: we cannot use electricity and radios and still believe that two people could be removed without harm from the belly of a wolf and be restored to life. In this regard the undeniable relationship to the story of Jonah proves Little Red Riding Hood to be a secondary construction. If the story has a historical root, one must painfully presume that the grandmother and the girl were in fact torn to bits by the wolf. No matter how one looks at it: Little Red Riding Hood was literally saved into the new life of *others* in Christian reality. The hunter is required only by the logic of the narrative— which sheds light on its obsolete secondary meaning. Henning Petersen pointed this out years ago in a subtle essay.

Thus the message of the Little Red Riding Hood story is clear: *Red Riding Hood's cause continues!* As a soteriological model, the story is an interpretation, indeed a compendium of existence in biblical faith. In it we recognize comfort and call, gift and commission, indicative and imperative, kerygma and paraenesis—in short, the transition from the old to the new eon into which we are transported. The New Testament scholar can only agree with the enlightened words of his colleague in systematics, who summarized the message of this story as follows (see above): "Little Red Riding Hood and the grandmother are thus shown to be paradigmatic figures representing the totality of human meaning transcending time and history, in which death and life, pain and joy, death and resurrection, action and reception, freedom and grace, kerygma and myth, existence and essence, individuality and sociality are dialectically mediated and yet paradoxically identical—that totality of human meaning, if I may so formulate it in conclusion, that is always prehended in the darkness of human questioning and *ap*-prehended in the dim light of faith, but is only *com*-prehended in the bright daylight of systematic-theological reflection."

To which bright daylight, however, as this investigation demonstrates, the New Testament scholar makes a weighty contribution!

Little Red Riding Hood:
A Perspective from Feminist Theology

Near the end of his Little Red Riding Hood commentary the New Testament colleague wants to emphasize ". . . that the story [of Little Red Riding Hood] also makes a clear statement about the woman question" (see the previous essay). What a typically ingratiating statement from a patriarch who wants to move with the times but still remain a patriarch! Feminist theologians will not be duped. The story of Little Red Riding Hood does not make *a* statement concerning the woman question, it is *the* statement regarding that question.

The New Testament scholar thinks that the father remains in the background? Little Red Riding Hood comes from a wholly patriarchal family. The hunter as a helper for life? The patriarch can never abstain from always drivelling about the importance of *his* "life"-giving importance! In fact, as will be seen, it is the figure of the hunter that represents a falsified patriarchal redaction of a story whose original ending was quite different. And the wolf as the epitome of evil? What defamation this peaceful creature, who eliminates the sick and perishing animals in an environmentally friendly manner, has had to endure! The wolf as the epitome of evil—such are the fantasies of men who have only one intention: to hold fast to the image of their fellow creature as inimical whenever this creature disputes the exclusive right of male persons to have the good creation at their exclusive disposal. No, it was entirely different. The story of Little Red Riding Hood is—both in its unfalsified historical root and in its literary form—the story of the emancipation of women.

Little Red Riding Hood thus came from a family dominated by her father, as was to be expected in the Late Middle Ages, when the historical core of this story originated. Even the name "Little Red Riding Hood" is a patriarchal euphemism of the redactor. The girl of course only showed herself "modestly" veiled, so as not to awaken anyone's desire for her father's "treasure." For the same reason, the father never let his daughter leave the house by herself. Her place in the family corresponded to the phallocentric hierarchy, with the structure discussed in the works of Corinna Redfern and Rosa Elisabeth Blackbird: husband → firstborn son → other sons → wife → daughters → men servants or apprentices → maidservants.

For historians of the Middle Ages it is a well-known fact that there were always women in the Middle Ages who, in spite of the prevalent discrimination against women, which was even internalized by most women, repeatedly made the most astonishing intellectual breakthroughs transcending the dominant ideology, and practical achievements in breaking out of the oppressive structures then in place. They did not accomplish their achievements with the proverbial "women's weapons," that is, their "man-killing" powers of seduction, the favorite excuse of those who have been surpassed by them. Instead they achieved through the inherent superiority of their insight and creative power. This was the case with Little Red Riding Hood. One day, when her father was away from the house and the sons and servants were out of earshot—thank goodness the "women's space" was taboo for men at the time!—the mother called her daughter and they discussed an ingenious plan. Little Red Riding Hood should visit her grandmother under the guise of a charitable deed, and deliberate with her the feasibility, so to speak, of a "tri-generational plan" for the liberation of women. The mother told her husband that the grandmother was sick, and ought to receive help by virtue of the Fourth Commandment. Therefore Little Red Riding Hood should bring her a strengthening supply of nutritious eco-bread (what else in the pre-industrial Middle Ages!) and freshly pressed wine, since at the moment she was unable to do for herself. The mother sought to refute the objection that it would be safer if one of the sons went with the not very conclusive argument that it concerned *her* mother, that is, Little Red Riding Hood's maternal grandmother. (At this point it is necessary to know that what androcentric Church history has failed to establish [see above: "Little Red Riding Hood in Church History"], women's scholarship has discovered: that the story deals with the maternal grandmother.) Of course the father was not convinced by this argument. He insisted that the strongest of the brothers must accompany Little Red Riding Hood on the dangerous path. The mother agreed, giving Little Red Riding Hood a subtle wink unnoticed by her husband.

So Little Red Riding Hood and her brother set out. On the unavoidable track through the forest they encountered a wolf. Here we must say something about method. In the literary history of the story the redactional falsification in the interest of the patriarchate begins at this point—or we should say, at this point *at the latest.* It was of course present earlier, but until this point the redactor only omitted important details (as described above). From this point on, however, he had to make blatant falsifications and rewrite the story with no regard for the truth. Only through the historical work of feminist scholarship, above all through its protagonist Lisa Gosswoman, has there been a breakthrough in very recent years. By applying the methods of literary criticism, as is common in biblical scholarship, she and other scholars have reconstructed the original form of the story and unmasked the redactional revisions for what they are: falsifications. After all of our experience with male scholarship it is hardly a surprise that it took so long. And still, it is a marvelous example of how the patriarchs in the end can be defeated with their own weapons.

So Little Red Riding Hood and her brother encountered the wolf. For Little Red Riding Hood this was no great shock. In spite of the misogynist societal context she, as a woman, had maintained her inner harmony with her fellow creatures. The wolf in turn had nothing evil in mind: he simply wanted to converse with Little Red Riding Hood. The brother reacted quite differently. In typical male fashion he was first seized by panic, and then his aggression was aroused. He picked up the largest branch on the ground and attacked the wolf. The animal, more defenseless than we usually think, took flight, the poorer in his expectations of communication with other creatures.

Nevertheless, Little Red Riding Hood had expected such a reaction, and had understood her mother's wink in just that sense. She took advantage of her brother's brief absence, while he chased the wolf, to shake him off and continue her way alone. First she picked a number of healing herbs—thus using the secret knowledge of wise women that her mother had shared with her and that, thanks to the stupidity of men, never passed beyond the doors of the women's quarters. Then she went on her way and arrived safely at her grandmother's. The wolf was already there, lying peacefully near her chair, having been fed with the scraps remaining from the grandmother's dinner. Little Red Riding Hood gave Grandmother her gifts and they discussed the "tri-generational plan." The plan required the support of women from all three generations, and proceeded in three steps: first, at the right moment they would destabilize the patriarchal structures of society (and the Church) through grassroots work in feminist theology. Next, by penetrating the male-dominated occupations, true to the old (pre-feminist!) slogan of "boring from within [the institutions]" they would occupy them. Finally they would overthrow those institutions and reestablish matriarchy. Men might still be able to keep down their wives and daughters, but they would not be able to withstand the concentrated rage of three generations. The wolf listened attentively to this strategy debate and considered his role as he recalled the incident with Little Red Riding Hood's brother. They ended by having a feast, and of course they invited the wolf.

And what about the business with the hunter who rescued Little Red Riding Hood and the grandmother from the belly of the wolf? Of course there is a slight historical basis, but the redactor has rendered it unrecognizable. Shortly after Little Red Riding Hood had left, her mother also managed to leave the house in an unwatched moment. Just as Little Red Riding Hood and Grandmother ended their conference the mother joined them and was warmly greeted. Naturally she did not intend to return home. Instead she preferred to wait with her own mother and daughter for the hour of liberation.

The father searched in vain for his wife the entire day. It did not cross his mind that she might be at Grandmother's. His ideas were more typically male: either she was committing adultery or she had entered a nunnery. When he did not find her, he died of grief. It was he, not the two women, who was the sufferer in this story. Even though his fate was deserved, one cannot repress a trace of compassion: Why was it impossible to achieve a new community of men and women? But no! The *redactor* shows the way out of the fix for androcentric posterity: The man searches and becomes the savior of the women!

In reality, Little Red Riding Hood and her mother and grandmother live on in the women of today. They *live* "God" in their holy relationship: on this point Dorothea Solo, Carter Heyman, and Elisabeth Schüssling-Firenze have said all that is necessary. When the hour comes (and it is already here) they will emerge from their hiding place and declare to the world the old and new message of joy about the God/ess of the Christian biblical tradition who has been revealed to *women*.

Little Red Riding Hood:
An Ecumenical Theology

Little Red Riding Hood was born of a marriage that united two confessions, as was already made clear by the canon lawyer in his description of the events (see his essay above). However, as a right-wing conservative hard liner who would have to worry about his job if any further ecumenical openness should occur, he spoke in the old manner of a *"mixed"* marriage, and he describes with relish all the spiritual and canonistic difficulties to which Little Red Riding Hood was subject on account of the "mixed marriage" of her parents, a kind of marriage "the Church vigorously opposed."

What the canon lawyer deliberately suppresses, however, are the many good and constructive experiences Little Red Riding Hood enjoyed in her confessionally varied parental household. Even though she was brought up a Lutheran by her mother, she always had great respect for the conscientiousness of her Catholic father. Everything that the parents could do together, they did: they read the Bible, and at the dinner table they discussed the differences between Luther's Bible and the German ecumenical common translation *("Einheitsübersetzung")*. They prayed together both from Luther's small prayerbook and from the Catholic hymnal and prayerbook, *Gotteslob*. They sang Lutheran chorales and Catholic hymns (and they were glad to find that many of these were contained in *Gotteslob*, with appropriate source citations—Luther's hymns being no longer concealed under the names of collections such as *Vehesches Gesangbuch* and the like). They never failed to attend an ecumenical worship service, but they were faithful to the restrictions imposed by their respective church leadership bodies. So it was that Little Red Riding Hood—who, after all, had been baptized a Catholic—received communion at the Catholic Mass without any difficulty; sometimes her mother did so, too, with the consent of the ecumenically-friendly Catholic pastor, while the father, faithful to the instructions of his Church, did not take part in the Lutheran celebration of the Lord's Supper. Of course the parents worked in the "Una Sancta" group in the nearest large city; it was one of the oldest such groups in the nation and was led by one of the best-known ecumenical theologians of the twentieth century. Thus they were not only intimately familiar with all the ecumenical problems, but they had also learned something that is essential to ecumenical dialogue: how to think in common with their fellow Christians from other churches, and to feel with their hearts in common with them, as well as suffering with them in and because of their respective churches.

For all these reasons it was simply a matter of course for Little Red Riding Hood to visit her grandmother frequently in her little house beyond the forest, because her father, faithful to the doctrines of the Council of Trent, had taught her to do good works for the love of God and to assist her fellow human beings. On the other hand, she had learned in religion class that it was a malicious lie to think, as some Catholics used to do, that "the Protestants" forbade good works and insisted on faith alone. On her way through the woods Little Red Riding Hood used to pass by an ancient chapel that now belonged to the Lutheran Church, and she was accustomed to decorating it with flowers she picked in the woods, for it had long been a thing of the past for a Protestant Christian to be jeered at as "Catholic" if she or he adorned a Protestant worship space, or even the altar, with flowers.

In short, Little Red Riding Hood lived in a soundly ecumenical world. Thus she and her parents were happy to adhere to the limits imposed by their respective churches because, on the basis of their good ecumenical experiences in family and church, they were convinced that all the old contradictions and enmities would soon be overcome, and the way to a new church community would be open to them. Important events and encouraging words from high, and even the highest, officials in both churches nourished their realistic hopes that important ecumenical steps would be taken before the year 2000.

But suddenly an utterly unexpected quarrel broke out: a merciless strife over divine mercy; an unjustified strife about justification; a wicked strife over sin; an idle strife over good works; a skeptical strife over faith; a church-dividing quarrel over the unity of the Church. The friends and defenders of ecumenical understanding were caught between two fires: the one side said that these ecumenists wanted (in their words) to spread "Gnostic ideas and the tenets of Freemasonry" and so to Protestantize the Catholic Church. The others said that the ecumenists wanted to bring the Protestant churches back under the rule of the Pope. Little Red Riding Hood was very sad about this, because she could not understand it at all. One day, when she was picking flowers for the Protestant chapel on her way to her grandmother's house, she was so depressed that she lay down on the forest floor and fell asleep.

She dreamed that a wolf rushed upon her and was about to devour her. In her dream she cried out, and the wolf stopped. Little Red Riding Hood said wonderingly: "What big ears you have!" "The better to hear what your so-called ecumenical theologians are spreading in the name of a so-called consensus," responded the wolf. "What big eyes you have!" cried Red Riding Hood again. "The better to see those who are making lazy theological compromises!" said the wolf. "And what a long nose you have!" "The better to smell the foul odor of plague that the Devil is spreading through Christianity," answered the wolf. "And what horrible big teeth you have!" "The better to crush all ecumenical weaklings," said the wolf, and Little Red Riding Hood dreamed that at that very moment the wolf seized her with his vicious teeth. She cried out again— and woke up. Beside her stood a Catholic student from her class at school, who had heard her crying out in her dream and awakened her.

Little Red Riding Hood realized that her sorrow over the developments in the ecumenical sphere had thrust her into a fearful nightmare. She was happy that it was only a dream, and immediately she placed the fate of ecumenism in the hands of the Holy Spirit, who would certainly bring about *his* hour and confirm the things of which she was already convinced.

We know that Little Red Riding Hood lived to be sixty-three years old (see the Epilogue below). She saw the year 2050, by which time the churches in the West had long since formed a new communion, and union with the Orthodox churches of the East was about to take place. The wise Pope John XXV had expressly declared that he claimed no jurisdiction over the other churches that wanted to join themselves to the Roman Catholic Church. His jurisdiction extended only to the Roman Catholic Church, as he was the patriarch of the oldest Western church. Even within his jurisdiction, he said, he would lay aside many of his traditional rights, in order to make the "freedom of Christian persons" more evident, and to create more trust in the Roman Church on the part of the other churches.

It was in that year 2050 that an extensive doctoral dissertation appeared, tracing and analyzing this process of church reunion and its theological bases in the pontificate of John XXV. It was accepted in the University of Hamburg, in the former department of Protestant theology—which in the mean time had been reorganized, on the model of American divinity schools, as interconfessional—and it was given the grade of *summa cum laude.* The person receiving the doctorate was, by the way, a great-grandson of a certain Otto Hermann Pesch, the grandson of Pesch's only daughter. This Pesch, a Catholic, had been a professor in the then-Protestant department of theology from the 1970s to the 1990s.

Little Red Riding Hood never studied theology but, recalling her youth, she struggled through the ponderous tome. All the while she was reading it she was thinking: "We already knew all that in 1999!"

Little Red Riding Hood:
A Pastoral Letter from the Bishop

Beloved Sisters and Brothers:

As everyone knows, there are many Christian men and women in our day who are troubled by the reality that faith and the Church are both losing influence and relevance in contemporary society. The secularism, liberalism, and individualism in our society, which our Holy Father, Pope John Paul II, has never wearied of lamenting in his apostolic letters in the past years, increasingly seduces people to seek only themselves. Possessions, success, profit, career, and a falsely-understood self-realization have become the highest goods. But since God, Jesus Christ, religion, Church, and the Christian life cannot easily be converted at face value into coin and market shares, the quest for them is failing, and human beings are becoming hardened against the appeal extended to them from the invisible reality of God. Before our eyes and ears, practical atheism and materialism are extending their grasp, those things of which the Second Vatican Council so prophetically spoke in the pastoral constitution "On the Church in the Modern World": humans "never enquire about God; religion never seems to trouble or interest them at all, nor do they see why they should bother about it" (§ 19). We Christians, who do not want to abandon God, are considered outmoded, eccentric, people of yesterday. Brothers and sisters, where is the challenging witness of faith that awakens that "troubling" over religion where it is absent, and shows that troubling its proper goal when it is aroused?

An event has come to our assistance that I label without hesitation as a gift of the Holy Spirit, who assists the Church until the end of the world (see Matt 28:20; John 16:13-15). You have all read, heard, or seen in the various media outlets in these last weeks the detailed reports concerning the deed of a young Christian woman who bore witness to her faith in exemplary fashion and in every respect serves as a model for us. I am speaking of the young woman whom I will refer to as "Little Red Riding Hood" in order to protect her anonymity. One can summarize the message of her Christian witness in three key sentences, which I would like to present for your reflection in this "Pastoral Letter for the Easter Season of Penance."

1. "Love Alone is Credible"

This dictum of the deceased theologian Hans von Melchior, whom the Holy Father deeply respected, could stand as a title for the deeds of Little Red Riding Hood. Credible first of all was her love for her parents. Not forced, but rather literally in the freedom of the children of God, that is to say out of love, she followed the instruction of her father and mother to show to her grandmother the service of love. This was therefore not only an act of love toward her grandmother, but first and foremost an act of obedience in the sense of the Fourth Commandment: you shall honor your father and mother. Indeed it was a heroic act of obedience! For it could only be enacted by the application of the virtue of courage, which the young woman needed in order to traverse the forest by herself. Who can fail to know, from watching current television programs, how dangerous the path through the forest in fact is? The necessary courage, which overcomes natural fear, could only be summoned by Little Red Riding Hood through a boundless trust in God, which bred in her an unshakeable hope in the God who has promised us that we are sheltered under his wings (Pss 36:8; 91:4).

She also evinced real love for her grandmother. It is not at all a banality that Little Red Riding Hood wanted to bring her something to eat and drink. Our society is as inimical to the elderly as it is to children. We sometimes forget how difficult it can be for the elderly to procure for themselves something to eat and drink. Together with her parents, Little Red Riding Hood fulfilled the elementary prerequisite of love, regarding which we are in full agreement with our Protestant brothers and sisters, despite the differences between our churches that still separate us: Little Red Riding Hood immersed herself in the *real* need of her neighbor, in this case her grandmother, and then acted decisively, which really improved her grandmother's situation. In addition, she prepared and packed everything in a pleasing manner because she knew—without need for a deeper theological theory—that people need not only material goods, but also signs of love, the "useless" gestures and symbols that desire only to express: I am fond of you, I love you, and I want you to be happy—or, in the words of the great Church doctor Thomas Aquinas: I want to be bound to you in friendship (see *ST* II-II 23,1).

Hence we see that Little Red Riding Hood gave such a convincing example of her faith that she had to actualize a great number of essential Christian virtues, and was able to do so, before she even took a step out of her parents' house.

2. Love is Always Endangered

We have all had to learn that it was not granted Little Red Riding Hood to travel the royal path of virtue unmolested to the end. For she lacked *one* virtue, the virtue of wisdom, although this can be pardoned on account of her tender age. Following the admonition of our Lord, "Be wise as serpents and innocent as doves" (Matt 10:16), Christian wisdom can differentiate between the false and correct means to an end. Little Red Riding Hood was luminously clear about the end of her Christian deed. But despite the virtue of love for God and neighbor instilled in her, the mother of all virtues (see *Catechism of the Catholic Church*, Nos. 1826-27), her youthful inexperience made it impossible for her to notice that straying from the designated path, even for the sake of a flower bouquet, could not be the proper means to her end. Who wants to fault the youngster, moved by the desire to complete and crown the sign of love through a bouquet of flowers from God's great nature? Little Red Riding Hood found herself in a genuine conflict of conscience, a weighing of the hierarchy of goods, for which she was not yet mature enough. Love was endangered to the degree that Little Red Riding Hood could become hesitant about yielding again to the courage to love.

Another failure was directly related to this moral lapse, and was indeed its verso: an exaggerated opinion of herself. Certainly this failure can be forgiven, since it did not result from a conscious decision to supplant the virtue of humility, as we would suspect to be the case with an adult Christian. No, childish inexperience was involved here also. We see from this that even under the rule of love one does not receive all the virtues simultaneously. Love is endangered since it must be learned for an entire lifetime and makes mistakes along the way.

Nevertheless, Little Red Riding Hood needed to examine her conscience at a later time, after everything had turned out well, to examine whether she had not lacked the proper attentiveness that was attainable even for a child of her age. As you know, dear sisters and brothers, every decision in conscience arises out of attentive testing of the manner in which the moral norm, proclaimed by the teaching office of the Church, is to be applied to a particular situation. The attention thus directed is a part of wisdom. This, the highest of the practical virtues, can only direct our conscientious decisions if we do not slacken in giving the necessary attention to the demands of the situation. A lack of attentiveness when it is demanded is a sin against wisdom. Therefore even the youthful conscience must be directed in a way adequate to it, so that it may never fail in the necessary attentiveness that is possible for it to attain. I do not hesitate to call this an integral element in a Christian upbringing, to which the parents have obligated themselves at their wedding and the godparents at the child's baptism. How else might we hope to have adult Christian men and women equipped with the virtue of Christian wisdom so integral for today's church and world?

Little Red Riding Hood first suffered the consequences of her inattentiveness herself. It is true that we must guard against the rash and all too hasty conclusion that God directly punished Little Red Riding Hood for her failures. What an image of our God, who is a God of Love (see 1 John 4:16), if we were to presume that he punished Little Red Riding Hood's youthful folly and inexperience immediately with death! And above all, on what grounds would he have punished the grandmother in addition? On the contrary, it is more than clear that precisely at this point there begins what I would like to call the supernatural meaning of the event, through which it becomes that witness to faith, indeed that splendid "demonstration of the Spirit and of power" (1 Cor 2:4), of which I spoke at the beginning. For therein Little Red Riding Hood's faith witness unites with God's answer. Our third core statement summarizes this witness:

3. Love is Stronger than Death

That Little Red Riding Hood's excusable and even unavoidable failure comes to a preliminary end with the attack of the insatiable wolf—first on the grandmother, then on the granddaughter—is so incomprehensible that disbelief here stands before simply unsolvable enigmas. But those who believe in God will immediately expect that the word of the Lord in John's gospel applies here as well: this has happened "so that God's works might be revealed" (John 9:3). It is not as though Little Red Riding Hood's love, insofar as it is a *human* act, overcomes death! But what is to be "revealed" is how *God* is shown to be salvific love to those who love selflessly. Therein God demonstrates to us that even our human love in all its faults is always sustained by the love of God that rules in all things.

There is another matter left for us to ponder in these events: God does not carry out his salvific work without us humans. There was need for the hunter in order that salvation might be drawn from a seemingly inevitable death. Just as God sent the man born blind to encounter our Lord Jesus Christ in order that, as we heard, "God's works might become revealed in him," so God sent the hunter along the path to the endangered grandmother and the defenseless child. God's wise arrangement is such that as followers of Jesus we should all hasten to the aid of our fellow human beings in the name of God.

One final note: it is no coincidence that the *hunter* becomes the rescuer, and not just anyone! What do I mean? The task required a *competent and expert* helper—in this case good will alone did not suffice. Our willingness to help others requires competence; it requires, to recall what was said earlier, not simply warm feelings, but wisdom and attentiveness as well.

Both the salvific help and the wisdom that makes this help efficacious—and with these thoughts I will conclude this reflection on the penitential Easter season—have an extensive ecumenical significance. As you know, our Holy Father, in his ecumenical encyclical *Ut unum sint* ("That They May Be One") of 1995, has placed the progress of ecumenical relations with our non-Catholic sister churches at the forefront of his concerns, not least in light of the approaching Holy Year 2000. The witness of faith and the doctrine derived from the events surrounding Little Red Riding Hood demonstrate a quite unique convergence, an agreement between the doctrine of our Catholic Church and the doctrine of our Lutheran sister churches. Martin Luther, the 450th anniversary of whose death in 1996 was commemorated with deep respect by the Catholic Church as well, was thoroughly convinced that pure faith always manifests itself in good works—indeed, as he said, must "take on flesh" in good works. He also and repeatedly said that in good works for our neighbor we "become another Christ." Finally, Luther insisted that our good works must *really* be good works; they must be such that they actually serve and help our neighbor—which again demands competence and attentiveness. These connections have been discovered and emphasized in recent decades especially through the work of Catholic Luther scholars. This at length invalidates an utterly ridiculous accusation that for a long time was raised in the Catholic Church against Lutheran teaching, namely that the Lutheran doctrine of *"sola fide"* promoted moral indifferentism.

Therefore, having said at the beginning that the events surrounding Little Red Riding Hood are a gift of the Holy Spirit to the Church, I may and must now add to this: they are a gift to ecumenism. We are all called in this penitential Easter season, in the spirit of these gifts, to make efforts toward a new community among the divided churches, and to work incessantly toward greater unity, so that, in light of God's actions for Little Red Riding Hood and her grandmother, the remaining differences between the churches may also be overcome.

May God give us his blessing for this purpose. And as a sign of this hope I wish all of you a blessed Easter season, and I give you my episcopal benediction.

† Clement
Bishop of Toptown

Little Red Riding Hood:
An Academic Treatment

Once upon a time[1] there was a sweet little lassie, and everyone who set eyes upon her loved her, not least her grandmother, who had no idea what all she ought to give this child.[2] One day the grandmother gave her a little hat made from red velvet, and since it looked so good on her, and she did not want to wear any other, she was henceforth called Little Red Riding Hood.[3] One day her mother said to her: "Come, Little

1. "Once upon a time" is the typical opening formula of the German fairy tale. The following text is derived from the 1812–1816 first edition of *Kinder- und Hausmärchen* by Jakob and Wilhelm Grimm, selected and introduced by Karl Rauch. Märchen europäischer Völker IV (Hamburg, Gütersloh, Stuttgart, Vienna, and Darmstadt, n.d.).

2. Probably unbeknownst to the editors, who were bound to the patriarchal tradition of the Enlightenment and Romantic periods, there is here a hidden indication of primeval matriarchal social structures even in the Germanic realm. On this see recently Alexander Mitscherlight, *The Motherless Society* (Frankfurt am Main, 1974) 1023–1467.

3. Little Red Riding Hood [Rotkäppchen] is the high German (that is, the Hannover dialect) form of the diminutive for Red Riding Hood [Rotkappe]. The *chen* corresponds to the Bavarian *erl*, the Swabian *le*, the Alemannian *li*, the Frankish *ele*, the Bohemian (and Austrian) *'l*, the Cologne *sche*, the Dutch *je*, and the Northern-Low German *ken*. The main character of our fairy tale is thus called " 's Rotkapperl" in Bavarian, " 's Rotkäpple" in Swabian, " 's Rotkäppli" in Alemannian, " 's Rotkäppele" in Frankish, " 's Rotkäpp'l" in Bohemian/Austrian, "et Ruutkäppsche" in the Cologne dialect, "het Rootkappje" in Dutch, and "dat Rotkäppken" in Northern-Low German. For the complicated linguistic relationships see the standard work by Horst Axelmann, *Das Diminutiv in den Weltsprachen. Unter besonderer Berücksichtigung des neutestamentlichen Griechisch und der deutschen Märchensprache [The Diminutive in the Languages of the World, with Special Attention to New Testament Greek and the Language of German Fairy Tales]* (Athens and Hamburg, 1988), especially §§ 17–21). Further specialized literature given in these paragraphs.

Red Riding Hood, here's a piece of cake and a bottle of wine. Bring them to your grandmother, for she is sick and weak, and these will refresh her.[4] Get going before it's too hot, and when you're out there, walk nicely and properly, without straying from the path. Otherwise you will fall and break the bottle, and Grandmother won't have anything. And when you get to her place, don't forget to say 'Good morning' and don't go snooping around in every corner first."[5]

"I'll take care of it," said Little Red Riding Hood, and shook hands on it.[6] However, the grandmother lived in the forest, half an hour from the village. As Little Red Riding Hood entered the forest, she encountered the wolf.[7] Little Red Riding Hood did not know what a vicious animal this was, and was not afraid of it.[8]

---

4. The naïve reference to cake and wine as a medicine to combat sickness and weakness reveals the pre-modern origins of the story. Since in addition, in 1 Tim 5:23, Paul implores his pupil Timothy to drink wine as a cure for stomach problems, in a purely Christian society reliance on this method is as much a matter of course as the seven days of creation. Of course the mother's worldview reveals nothing of the practical rationality of the modern sort. On this see Klaus-Gabriel Kodaillé, *Lust und Last der Zweckrationalität. Eine Untersuchung im Anschluß an Søren Kierkegaard [The Pleasure and Burden of Calculated Rationality. An Investigation after Søren Kierkegaard]* (Hamburg and Hofgeismar, 1991).

5. Here one cannot help but notice the repressive structure of the (putative) family in the Late Middle Ages and its destructive, fear-arousing, trust-blocking effect on the adolescent psyche. See the analytic and therapeutic as well as ingenious interpretation by Edmund Dräuermann, *Das unbekannte Rotkäppchen. Psychogramm einer Kindertragödie [The Unknown Red Riding Hood. Psychogram of a Childhood Tragedy]* (Paderborn, 1992). This study instigated a worldwide discussion of the matter.

6. The Hanseatic gesture of the handshake to seal a matter should not tempt us to draw premature conclusions about the *Sitz im Leben* of the story. Too many factors suggest an origin other than Northern Germany. See the helpful remarks in the above essay on Church history.

7. See also Dräuermann, 280–364: "Das Wolf-Symbol—Archetyp des angsterzeugten und angsterzeugenden Über-Ich" ("The Wolf Symbol: Archetype of the fear-induced and fear-inducing Superego").

8. There has been fierce dispute among scholars about whether here one should think, as was earlier supposed, of Paul Tillich's "dreamlike innocence" or, with more recent interdisciplinary scholarship, of a distant

"Good morning, Little Red Riding Hood," he said.

"Thank you very much, wolf."

"Where are you going so early, Little Red Riding Hood?"[9]

"To Grandmother's."

"What've you got under your apron?"

"Cake and wine: yesterday we baked, and I am supposed to bring my weak, sick grandmother something to eat, which will give her strength."[10]

"Where does your grandmother live, Little Red Riding Hood?"

"Another fifteen minutes through the woods. Her house is under the three large oak trees. The nut hedges are just below it. You'll recognize it," said Little Red Riding Hood.

The wolf thought to himself, "This young, tender thing is a nice piece of meat. She'll taste better than the old one. You must think of something cunning so you can get both of them."

They walked along together for a few minutes, and then the wolf said, "Little Red Riding Hood, look at the pretty flowers all around us. Why don't you look around? I don't think you even hear how sweetly the birds are singing! You are just walking along as if you were on the way to school, and it's so nice

---

echo of a holistic worldview and the harmony of humanity with its "older siblings," the animals. The latter thesis depends on a fundamental insight: as with humans, so with animals. In other words, the wolf is only "a vicious animal" because people consider it to be so, thereby making it so, and reacting to it accordingly (we must be precise in saying "supposedly" reacting, because in reality human beings only sow what they reap). Obviously it is impossible at this stage to settle this lively debate.

9. Notice the significant reference to the time of day, mentioned here for the first time! Since the grandmother only lives thirty minutes from the village, scholars are faced with a question: should one assume that since Little Red Riding Hood was going to "refresh" her, the grandmother was used to drinking wine in the morning? One could only interpret such behavior as that of an alcoholic. Or perhaps this reference exposes different layers of redaction. In light of the pedagogical intention of the fairy tale, the latter seems more plausible, since an author with pedagogical intentions would scarcely have portrayed the grandmother, who is otherwise painted as inspiring trust, as an alcoholic. Still, the intention of the later redactor, who was apparently insensitive to pedagogical requirements, remains a mystery.

10. See the remarks in n. 4!

out here in the woods."[11] Little Red Riding Hood lifted her eyes, and when she saw how the sunbeams danced among the trees and how the ground was sprinkled with beautiful flowers she thought to herself, "If I bring Grandmother a fresh bouquet it will make her very happy. It is so early in the morning that I can get there in plenty of time anyway."[12] She left the path and went into the woods to look for flowers. Every time she plucked one she saw another, farther on, that seemed even more beautiful; so she wandered deeper and deeper into the forest.[13] The

11. The entire dialogue, concluding with the wolf's reproaches, is a typical component of a fairy tale for which the "historical-critical school" of fairy tale scholars—the natural opponents of the psychoanalytical school represented by Edmund Dräuermann—has invented the descriptive concept of "virtual projective transformation-extrapolation." It is "virtual" because in its own time the dialogue only proceeds opportunistically, and then later receives a verbal form in the narrative recollection. It is "projective" because it imagines inner feelings and fears as external events and takes them for realities. The "transformation" stems from the fact that the dialogue originally exists in the realm of feeling and is only transformed secondarily into words and concepts. Finally, it is an "extrapolation" because the inner reality in the medium of the transformative projection now in fact becomes a quasi-external reality that actually works backward through the plot toward the inner event, as the course of the story confirms. In light of this concept Little Red Riding Hood's original emotions and fears can be reconstructed through careful examination of the text (the zeal for accumulation of information for the sake of self-appeasement, in the end the supposed shared knowledge with the wolf, etc.). For a comprehensive overview see Fulko Steven Sky, *Projective Reality. A Key Notion for the Analysis of Fairy-Tales* (London, New York, and Disneyland, 1985).

12. In contrast to the previous "dialogue," these "thoughts" of Little Red Riding Hood are a normal "inner monologue"—"normal" because we find it in some of the parables of Jesus as well as in classic German drama. It appears to be a stylistic element characteristic of European culture, indicating its introversion and self-fixation. See François Vougénot, *Le monologue interne depuis les paraboles de Jésus jusqu'au drame classique allemand. Une étude diachrone socio-psychologique de la culture Européenne [The Internal Monologue, from the Parables of Jesus to Classical German Drama. A sociopsychological diachronic study of European culture]* (Paris and Lausanne, 1984).

13. Here one should note, as was stated in the missiological version of the Little Red Riding Hood story, that the flowers, despite the poetic description, "brought happiness" first and foremost as herbs, and not as decorations. This could explain a certain redundancy in Little Red Riding

wolf, however, went directly to the grandmother's house and knocked on the door.

"Who's there?"

"Little Red Riding Hood. Open up; I've brought you cake and wine."

"Just turn the handle," called the grandmother. "I am too weak and can't get up."[14]

The wolf pressed on the handle and the door opened. Without saying a word, he went directly to the grandmother's bed and devoured her.[15] Then he changed into her clothes, put on her bonnet, laid himself in her bed, and drew the curtains.[16]

Hood's efforts to gather more and more flowers. In the times before pharmaceutical science, quantity replaced quality.

14. It might appear that in the dialogue between the grandmother and the wolf we have another example of the virtual projective transformation-extrapolation mentioned in n. 11. This is not the case, however, for two reasons: first, the grandmother does not see the wolf, and thus cannot harbor any fears, nor assimilate such fears in a projectively verbalized manner. Second, as opposed to the situation of Little Red Riding Hood, the dialogue does not result in a psychic movement that remains internal, and that, together with its motive, would become the object of projective verbalization. Instead, it remains an event in the psychic outerworld: the door opens, as will soon be apparent. Here we are dealing with a real, non-verbal communication whose original course can no longer be reconstructed, and with the performative content of this discourse. The verbalization results from someone outside, most likely the hunter, who arrived later, and not from the subject of the action. In such cases scholarship speaks of a real, non-verbal performative dialogic potentiality. See Sky, *Projective Reality* 547–761.

15. "Without saying a word"—even the fairy-tale literary form reveals, like an involuntary reflex, the reality that animals by their nature differ essentially from *homo sapiens sapiens* in that they lack the ability to speak. Moreover, once certain exaggerations that are common to fairy tales are removed, the account is entirely plausible when one realizes that, according to burial finds, physical acceleration had not yet begun: human beings therefore were smaller, and the sick grandmother should be thought of as quite fragile, while animals had not yet experienced the evolutionary reduction of their body mass (cf., for example, the reduction of dinosaurs to lizards). Therefore a gigantic wolf of that time could have "devoured" an old, fragile adult plus a young child.

16. If the remarks in the previous footnote are accurate the next part of the text can only be regarded as literary stylization. The grandmother's

Meanwhile, Little Red Riding Hood was collecting flowers. When she could carry no more she remembered her grandmother and again set out to find her.

Little Red Riding Hood was surprised to find the doors open, and when she entered the room it looked so strange[17] that she thought to herself, "Ah,[18] my God, I feel so anxious today, and normally I enjoy being at Grandmother's."

She called, "Good morning!" but heard no response. She went to the bed and opened the curtains. Grandmother lay in bed with her bonnet pulled down over her face, which seemed very strange.[19]

"Ah,[20] Grandmother, what big ears you have!"[21]

"The better[22] to hear you with."

"Ah, Grandmother, what big eyes you have!"

"The better to see you with."

---

clothes could not have fit the wolf, and the wolf could not have fit in her bed. Most likely the ill-disposed wolf became hopelessly entangled in the fabrics in the grandmother's bedroom. This would also explain Little Red Riding Hood's bewilderment.

17. Aha! See the previous note.

18. This is an older expression of shock, but also expresses ridicule and admonition (although these are not applicable here). We should not confuse it with the French "*Ai!*"—an expression of sudden pain (in English "Ow!"). "Ah" in this context is synonymous with the equally ancient "O!", in English and American "Oh!", in ancient Greek "*idou,*" in Latin "*ecce!*", in Italian "*ecco!*", in American Indian "How!", among the youth "Super!" in the sense of "Awesome!"

19. Here one should note that Little Red Riding Hood has only an instinctive presentiment of the wolf, but does not recognize him rationally! One can credit this fact to the special tension between a clear and very real feeling that engenders fear and blind reason that negates reality—according to the secondary intention of the author no doubt a symbol of the eternal *conditio humana* (i.e., the essential condition of the human being). Only the reader can feel "enlightened," like the audience at a detective film, in which the viewers are more intelligent than the actors on the screen.

20. See n. 18.

21. "What . . ." is an archaic variant of "Why do you have . . ." and has since become a regular part of colloquial speech.

22. Combined with "What . . . ," this is still a grammatically incorrect formulation of "So that." It is grammatically correct only in a consecutive clause with "Why do you have such. . . ."

"Ah, Grandmother, what big hands you have!"

"The better to grab you with."

"But grandmother, what horribly big teeth you have!"

"The better to eat you with."[23]

As soon as the wolf had said this, he leapt from the bed and devoured[24] poor Little Red Riding Hood.

So[25] the wolf had appeased his cravings; he went back to bed, fell asleep, and began snoring loudly.[26] The hunter[27] was just passing the house and thought: "As loud as that old woman is snoring, you ought to see if there is something wrong with her." He entered the room, and when he got near the bed he

23. The remarks in n. 11 apply in principle to the above dialogue between Little Red Riding Hood and the wolf with two important exceptions: first, in the *ductus* of the story Little Red Riding Hood's questions are genuine—and understandable! (see n. 16). Only the wolf's answers are "projective reality" (Sky). Second, in light of the organic structure of the human subject, together with the dramatic apogee indicated in the final question, the sequence of questions and answers apparently serves not only to verbalize Little Red Riding Hood's projections, but also to represent the increasing hungers of the wolf—we might say his non-verbal projections in the medium of an extrapolation transformative of Little Red Riding Hood. Thus Little Red Riding Hood's virtual projective transformation-extrapolation, her inner monologue, and the wolf's projections, which are non-verbal, but transformable through human intervention, are combined in a successful literary climax. Scholars have coined the term "rational symbiotic representation" to describe this synthesis. This proves, among other things, that projections must by no means be divorced from reality and the potentiality for reality, as is demonstrated in the remainder of the narrative.

24. See n. 15.

25. Colloquial children's language in the sense of "when." This construction is not without a substantial legitimation in the Latin *"ubi"* in the sense of "as soon as." Which means that we advise not correcting high school students who use "so" in this sense!

26. The two previous sentences constitute the tragic climax of the story, after which, according to the rules of classical drama, the turn toward the good must follow. In this case the shift is introduced by a "satirical moment": the wolf's snoring inaugurates the ensuing action.

27. Why not *a* hunter? We must conclude from this nuance that in those times there already existed a preliminary form of the present-day office of "forester" with a monopoly on hunting.

saw the wolf lying there. "Here you are, you old rascal," he said. "I've been looking for you for a long time."[28] He was about to shoot the wolf with his gun, but then it occurred to him that the wolf might have eaten the grandmother, and that she might still be saved. Instead of shooting, he took a pair of scissors and began to cut open the belly of the sleeping wolf.[29] After he had made a small incision, he saw the red hood glowing, and after another couple of snips the girl jumped out and cried, "Oh, was I scared! It was so dark inside the body of the wolf!"[30] Next appeared the old grandmother. She was still alive but could hardly breathe.[31] Little Red Riding Hood quickly fetched several heavy stones and put them in the wolf's stomach. When he awakened he tried to run away, but the stones were so heavy that he immediately sank back and fell down dead.[32]

28. The entire catastrophe of the inter-zoological relationship between human and wolf is encapsulated in this sentence. Hermann Piscator analyzes this catastrophe with a sure mastery of methodology in *Der Wolf: dein Freund und Begleiter. Geschichte einer Katastrophe unter besonderer Berücksichtigung der Theologie Friedrich Schleiermachers. [The Wolf: Your Friend and Companion. History of a Catastrophe, with Special Attention to the Theology of Friedrich Schleiermacher]* 2 vols. (Kiel, Hamburg, and Heidepark, 1981–86). See also the interpretation by the church historian in the chapter "Little Red Riding Hood in Church History" in the present volume.

29. This passage not only attests to mental alertness, but also to the skilled technical competence of the hunter. For if the first incision had not killed the wolf, the consequences for the remainder of the event would have been incalculable!

30. Obviously Little Red Riding Hood still did not grasp the processes of projection and extrapolation. She misunderstood her time in the belly of the wolf as a problem with the lighting.

31. The grandmother's accumulated experience and familiarity with the dangers of the forest did not allow her to entertain any illusions. She understood the real problem, namely the limited amount of oxygen! It is not difficult to imagine the predicament if one has ever been trapped in an elevator! The above remark also verifies the narrow time period of the event. The wolf must have started snoring *immediately,* and the hunter must have been led to the grandmother's house *at once* by Lady Luck. This once again proves *a posteriori* the excess of the wolf's lustful hungers.

32. Obviously a literary pleonasm to achieve dramatic assurance of a happy ending to the story! For as we convincingly demonstrated in n. 29,

All three were satisfied.[33] The hunter skinned the wolf and went home with the hide. Grandmother ate the cake and wine that Little Red Riding Hood had brought and was refreshed. But Little Red Riding Hood thought to herself: "For the rest of your days you shall not stray from the path and run through the forest when your mother has forbidden it."[34]

---

the wolf must have been dead already. The logical inconsistency is indicated by the fact that the wolf could not spring to his feet, and therefore could *not* have "fallen down dead," but only "sank back,"—which makes it hard to understand why he then died.

33. The choice of the world "satisfied" [German "vergnügt"] conjures up a delectable feature of the old German language. Being "satisfied" means having "enough," or having "one's fill" in the sense of attaining the sum of life's meaning, to borrow an expression of my colleague in systematic theology. It is thus the exact opposite of "pleasure" [German "Vergnügen"] = diversion and amusement. The Baroque period still preserved the immense value of this word. Recall Johann Sebastian Bach's Cantata, "Ich habe genug!" ["I have enough!"]. The formulation in the Little Red Riding Hood story brings to mind in dramatic fashion the phenomenon of the corruption of the language. In its full sense the word "enough" only appears in theological language games, when one speaks of the "enoughness" of Scripture. Even in this case one increasingly sees the technical word "sufficiency" in its place.

34. Little Red Riding Hood later confirmed the conclusion insinuated by the narrator: she never had another opportunity to test her steadfastness in following her good intentions. See her account in the "Epilogue in Heaven" below.

Epilogue in Heaven:
A Conversation Between Little Red Riding Hood and the Apostles Peter and Paul, with Jesus Christ Joining In at the End

Location: In Heaven. A comfortable but by no means lavishly decorated room intended for good conversation and indispensable writing tasks, with a corner sofa on the right and a desk on the left by a window wall looking down to the earth. A folding door in the background.

Time: Eternity, but in the mode of eternity simultaneous with the year 1523 (see above: "Little Red Riding Hood in Church History").

Peter is seated at his desk examining various files and occasionally glancing dreamily at the earth.

Paul (entering through the door): Good morning, brother ancient apostle!

Peter (turning around slowly in his chair): You've forgotten your dogmatics again, brother Apostle of the Gentiles! In our eternity there is neither morning nor evening!

Paul: Okay. Then good eternal now! In any case: all good wishes! Do you approve?

Peter (slightly grumpy): Please, a bit more dogmatic seriousness. But let it go. In your case it's all love's labors lost on that subject. What's up?

Paul: We're getting an addition.

Peter: One of your people?

Paul: Anachronistic nonsense! Look at the earth! It is 1523 down there. It's a Catholic woman.

Peter: Now *I* have to say: no anachronistic insinuations! My people have enough to suffer under my successors—check that—under those who consider themselves my successors! Who is she?

Paul: She is a lady whom people could never get out of the habit of calling by a name that got attached to her when she was a little girl: "Little Red Riding Hood."

Peter: Her age?

Paul: According to earthly years, sixty-three. According to our calendar .0063 of a day, but I do not need to remind an assiduous dogmatician of the reference to Psalm 90:4. (Winks) For once we are in agreement against Dr. Martin Luther, that it is not "a prayer of Moses," am I right?

Peter (somewhat absent-mindedly): Oh, yes, the good Dr. Martinus. God grant him . . . . (Suddenly very alert): Is he here?

Paul: Of course! That is to say, not yet according to earthly calculation, but that doesn't matter to us! Don't worry; he'll wait till you're ready before he introduces himself. Even eternity has its *kairos* when necessary! But back to the lady. . . .

Peter: . . . I want to see her!

Paul: Madam!

Little Red Riding Hood (entering): Glory be to the Father and. . . .

Peter (interrupting): Here every breath praises God. You no longer need to carry out a formal rite.

Little Red Riding Hood (relieved): Thank God! I have always thought: doesn't God already know how we really want to praise him? (After a short, astonished pause): I never thought things would be so relaxed up here.

Paul: You will have to change your thinking about a lot of things up here. But I assure you that you will enjoy shucking off all the stuff that you poor Christian people were indoctrinated with under the auspices of my brother apostle (pointing to Peter).

Peter: For once brother Apostle of the Gentiles is right. I don't want to be in the theologians' heaven, the one they have set up as it ought to be, and where they think I am.

Those good, zealous people really have produced too much of a good thing. They even managed to discover a concept of the triune God. However, that was the secret knowledge of highly trained theologians. You were spared, and at most had esoteric sermons about it preached over your heads on Trinity Sunday.

Paul: My people were more careful later on. I was always a specialist in the unknowable and the unutterable. Have you ever read the thirteenth chapter of my letter to the Corinthians?

Little Red Riding Hood: You wrote to the Corinthians, too?

Paul: You didn't know that?

Little Red Riding Hood: No, I really didn't. I never learned to read, and in church the priests always read from the Bible in Latin. The pastor preached in German, but he only talked about the Gospel.

Paul: Now I am really flabbergasted. Even in heaven we live and learn. I made such an effort with the Corinthians. I wrote several long letters to those thickheaded people —I forget if it was two or three. I will have to ask Rudi Bultmann; he seems to know everything.

Little Red Riding Hood (somewhat confused): Rudi Who-mann? Excuse me, but this is a little too fast for me. I only wanted to know why things are so relaxed here.

Paul (eagerly): It has a lot to do with Rudi Bultmann—I mean, with my first letter to the Corinthians. . . . It's about hermeneutics, you see.

Little Red Riding Hood: Her-new-ma-tics? What is that?

Paul: Her-me-neu-tics is when someone understands an old story and thereby blends the horizon of his or her own experience with that of the people in the story. Thus one also calls hermeneutics the "blending of horizons."

Little Red Riding Hood: Oh, is that it!

Peter (in a pedagogic-religious tone): Brother Paul means that people always make their own image of how things are, but they all mean the same thing.

Paul: Well stated, brother. Now if only your people could say it so simply!

Little Red Riding Hood: I still don't understand. The priests told me I would sit in a red-upholstered chair and sing hymns all day long. Now I am here and it is completely different. So the priests' preaching was all wrong. Is that because of her-new-mat-ics?

Peter: Little Red Riding Hood is giving us food for thought, which is fine with me.

Paul (somewhat annoyed): The good child can't know any better. But at least *you* should have grasped something of a multidimensional concept of truth.

Peter: As far as I am concerned, it can be five-dimensional! But hermeneutics or no hermeneutics (turns to the desk), I have here some copies of a manuscript by someone called Otto Hermann Pesch. He must have been a theologian with too much free time. He searched everywhere and throughout the ages for stories about Little Red Riding Hood, and came across a whole lot of them. They are so different that they could not possibly all be true. You have to wonder, damn it (stops in consternation and turns his eyes upward)—Sorry!—how it really was!

Paul: *That* is "hermeneutic appropriation!" All the authors worked within their own horizon of understanding, and reformulated it accordingly. Your people do the same with dogmas, and then call it *"relecture."*

Peter: But now I want to know how it really was.

Paul: Oh, all right, if you are so obsessed with naked factual truth! Let's just ask Little Red Riding Hood ourselves!

Peter (beckoning Little Red Riding Hood over to the desk): Here, read this manuscript quickly! You can read all by yourself now!

Little Red Riding Hood (skimming the pages, and gradually beginning to roar with laughter; by the end she cannot stop laughing): This (can't go on because she is laughing so hard) is supposed to be (laughs) my story?

Peter and **Paul** (flabbergasted, in chorus): What?

Peter: Let's sit down (pointing to the sofa) and make ourselves comfortable. Then Little Red Riding Hood can tell us the story from the beginning.

Little Red Riding Hood (waiting respectfully until Peter and Paul are seated comfortably in their upholstered chairs. She sits on a chair between them, but teeters timidly on the front edge of the cushion): Okay, that part about the baked goods and wine for my grandmother is true. I used to visit my grandmother regularly, and there was nothing peculiar about it. Once, however, on an unusually beautiful day, I noticed some wonderful wildflowers in the woods. Since I had time, I picked some. My parents never forbade this; on the contrary, they always told me: if you find something useful in the forest that would make Grandmother happy, take it with you!

Peter: Then the wolf did not lead you astray?

Little Red Riding Hood (roaring with laughter again): The wolf? I just read about him for the first time, and now I understand some things better! What was unique about that day was in fact an animal, but it was a *deer*, not a wolf (shaking with laughter once again). A cute little deer! We made friends right away. It went with me to Grandmother's, and never left our side.

Paul (as if to himself): I must tell this to my sister apostle Junia. She will put on her finest feminist smile!

Little Red Riding Hood: Then Grandmother and I did do something improper—and I have paid a heavy enough price for it. We decided to keep the deer with us for a few days. We lived together for eight days, and then the deer ran back to its herd. I parted from Grandmother, not realizing that I had seen her for the last time. For after that incident my parents would not let me visit her any more. Later I understood why. They were really afraid that I was dead. It did not occur to my parents or to the neighbors, who were also worried, that I had simply stayed with my grandmother. They just couldn't imagine that I would act so independently, so they thought something had happened to me. That must be how the story with the wolf got started. It's really silly! Wolves do not attack people as long as they can find enough sick animals and carcasses, and there are plenty of those in the forest.

After that I stayed at my parents' house and from then on was a good, obedient little daughter. When I ventured into the streets, however, everyone kept their distance from me. The times were hard, and my parents were very poor. I had long been eligible for marriage, but nobody wanted to take me as a bride, or, to put it bluntly, nobody *could* marry me, although a few young men fell in love with me. In those days the parents had the last word, and they always said: she will run away from you just as she ran away from her parents!

So I got to be twenty-two, and was considered an "old maid" for those days. It must have been the year 1482 by my reckoning. I became a Beguine—what other options were there?! Your people, Peter, nearly burned me at the stake for it, since they thought we were all witches. Thank goodness there were a few reasonable people who fought for my release.

Peter (nods hard and shoots Paul a significant look).

Little Red Riding Hood: That is my whole story. In the last few years, beginning around 1518, there was a great amount of unrest. I never really understood why it was all such a big deal, but I did think it was a good thing that the people did not have to give their entire savings to buy a letter of indulgence. I died peacefully, and now I am here.

Peter and **Paul** are silent for a long time. Meanwhile the folding door opens silently, unnoticed by the three of them, and Jesus Christ enters. When Little Red Riding Hood, Peter, and Paul finally catch sight of him they jump up and all cry out:

Peter and **Paul** (in unison): Teacher!

Little Red Riding Hood: Oh, so *that* is how you look!

Jesus (lifting his hands defensively): One at a time! My dear, faithful disciples and apostles, I could almost hold it against you, after I explained it to you so often! My good witness Matthew beat it into you that I once said: "You are not to be called teachers, for you have one teacher, the Messiah" (Matt 23:10). Unfortunately in those times there were not such good biblical scholars as today. Still—Rudolf Bultmann, to name only one, has brought it to your attention that I was not making a canon for Church law. Instead I only meant to warn you not to imitate the Scribes and Pharisees. As for how we should relate to one another, you should believe (at last!) what my true witness John handed down from me: "I have called you friends, because I have made known to you everything that I have heard from my Father" (John 15:15). In all seriousness, don't you want to get it right, finally?

Peter: Yes, Friend-Teach . . .

Paul (interrupting): Yes, Friend Jesus!

Jesus (hugging Little Red Riding Hood): And now for you! They almost all say that when they arrive: "Oh, that is how you look!" You will have fun changing your image of me! Against their own intention, your great painters provided for an inevitable surprise, which is very nice. So I really can't be angry with them.

Little Red Riding Hood (timidly): Do I have to go to choir practice right away?

Jesus (laughing): Your theologians and preachers must have taught you that! Unlike the painters, sometimes I really want to get angry with those guys—if I could do that here! What utter nonsense they told you sometimes!—and really everything was and is so easy. No, you do not have to go to the choir, and certainly not to practice. Here nobody "has to" do anything. You should sing if and when your heart desires, but only voluntarily!

Little Red Riding Hood: Praise be to God! I always liked singing voluntarily, but was rarely allowed to do so. Thus (timidly) I often did it in secret.

Jesus: I know! I always enjoyed watching what you did on earth, even and especially when people thought you had kicked over the traces and were behaving "improperly." For example, the incident with your grandmother, the flowers, and the deer: that was risky, and somewhat inconsiderate toward your parents. Still, you followed a good instinct and discovered wonderful things that a "good girl" does not find out—at least not so young.

Little Red Riding Hood (with an audible sigh of relief): Then you are not angry with me?

Jesus: On the contrary. For your courage in going your own way—and not only that time—you shall have a place of honor (as long as you don't run through heaven singing the way you did through the forest)!

Little Red Riding Hood: But I am nothing special.

Jesus: Precisely! I was always for the so-called "little ones."

Peter (somewhat shyly, and conscious of the risk): But Friend Jesus, everything that is right . . . . Have you considered the pedagogical effects if this were known on earth?

Jesus: Can you ever stop trying to be such a know-it-all? (Laughs mischievously.) But don't worry, my dear friend, I won't tell you again, "Get behind me, Satan" (Mark 8:33).

Peter (lowering his head and mumbling almost inaudibly): Yes, Friend Jesus.

Jesus (turning to Little Red Riding Hood): As you know from your catechism, I sit (so far as I sit at all) "at the right hand of the Father." The place next to me, as you also know, belongs to my dear mother Mary. However, she rarely sits there. She is busy most of the time, traveling around heaven, and she enjoys spending time with my friends when she is not looking after my faithful on earth. My twelve apostles sit next to us, that is, when they are not off somewhere else, as Paul and Peter are just now, because they are welcoming you. I already promised them that (Luke 22:30). But I only promised them *that* they would sit with me at table, on their thrones. I did not say which *particular* seats they would have. So I think they will move back to make space for you. The seating arrangement at table in the reign of God from now on will be as follows: my mother Mary next to me, then Little Red Riding Hood, then Peter and the other apostles, and finally, since there must be order, Paul as the thirteenth apostle. But on certain earthly feast days Paul will sit between Little Red Riding Hood and Peter, at the head of all the apostles, and that will be the case every Sunday, because he wrote so profoundly about my resurrection from the dead, and on the feast days of the great missionaries, for instance Ansgar, Boniface, Corbin, Cyril and Methodius, Francis Xavier, and many others, since Paul preached my gospel so tirelessly to the Gentiles. Peter will sit between Mother Mary and Little Red Riding Hood on the feast days on which the events of my life are celebrated, because he was the first to confess me, and did so on behalf of all others.

So now let us celebrate our new community!

Peter, Paul, and **Little Red Riding Hood** look at each other speechlessly. Jesus suddenly disappears, as quietly as he had arrived. Finally:

Paul: Whenever HE has been here I have to take a deep breath. How everything always comes to him so naturally . . . !

Peter: I know what you mean about "taking a deep breath." It was always that way when we were going around with him, when *you* (slight tone of triumph in his voice) were not yet with us.

Paul (a bit grumpy): Thank you very much for so elegantly reminding me of my past life. But I will generously refrain from trading barbs.

Little Red Riding Hood: Well, *I* don't have to take a *deep* breath. I can just *exhale,* finally; because now that I am *in* heaven I can really take delight in it. I like the way it is here.

Paul: Madam, Brother Ancient Apostle, I suggest we take a break, a nice long break appropriate to eternity, and have a look at the earth.

Peter: You mean we should switch to the year 2000?

Paul: Exactly.

Little Red Riding Hood: Oh yes, I am madly curious!

All three take their chairs from the corner and push the desk away from the window wall so that they can put their chairs right in front of the window. All three sit down—even Little Red Riding Hood now sinking back into the upholstery—and look down at the earth. What they see truly amazes them. They can't be sad any more, because they know that in the end God will restore everything and make right what God's children have spoiled. It is no longer necessary to get upset. But to be astonished: that is possible and appropriate.

Peter, Paul, and Little Red Riding Hood often sit by the window and gaze at what occurs on earth throughout the earthly years. They see all the things that people think they should do and not do, supposing they are doing God a service. The three observers in heaven can only marvel at all of this. And they go on marveling, as long as the beautiful blue planet still turns on its axis each day and goes on revolving around the sun.

Postscript to the Revised Third Edition

Between the second and third editions of this book the fairy tale teller, thanks to the generous communication of the author, became acquainted with Hans Ritz's book, *Die Geschichte vom Rotkäppchen. Ursprünge, Analysen, Parodien eines Märchens* (11th rev. and expanded ed. Kassel: Muriverlag, 1993).

He was shocked to discover what an illustrious company his theological jokes about Little Red Riding Hood had joined. Above all, he finally discovered who had invented "Little Red Riding Hood in German Bureaucratese." He could at last give credit where credit is due: to Thaddäus Troll (see Ritz, *Geschichte* 141–42). In addition, the text, or at least that portion of the text cited, was compared with the original and corrected where necessary, for the anonymous copies being circulated were in some sections considerably distorted. But how Thaddäus Troll —a well-known name in "academic circles" and especially to theology professors—could fall so quickly and thoroughly into anonymity remains a mystery. In an analogous situation biblical scholarship would employ all the methods of "form-critical" and "tradition-critical" research to crack the case. Meanwhile Hans Ritz solved the puzzle himself in the twelfth edition of his book (Kassel, 1997, pp. 237–39). The book is highly recommended reading—for the story itself is a satire that well withstands comparison with the satiric original!

1 January 1998   Otto Hermann Pesch

Glossary

Axelmann, Horst: = Axel Horstmann, Assistant Professor of New Testament Greek in Hamburg.

Blackbird, Rosa Elisabeth: = Rosalies Taube, feminist theologian. Holds the doctorate in systematic theology. Lecturer in feminist theology and pastor in Lübeck.

Bultmann, Rudi: = Rudolf Bultmann, Professor of New Testament in the Protestant faculty of theology in Marburg; with Karl Barth one of the two most influential Protestant theologians in Germany in the 1950s and 1960s. Specialties: New Testament form criticism, Gospel of John, "demythologizing," and "existential interpretation." D. 1976.

Cobbs, Theodosius: = Theodor Ahrens, Professor of Missiology and Ecumenical Relations of the Churches, Hamburg. Specialties: Melanesia, Papua New Guinea.

Corneeling, Paul: = Peter Cornehl, Professor of Practical Theology, Hamburg. Specialties: Homiletics, History and Theology of Worship.

Dräuermann, Edmund: = Eugen Drewermann, widely read German psychotherapist and theologian. Specialties: Biblical interpretation and revision of the dogmatic tradition from the point of view of depth psychology and psychotherapy.

Enomyia-Lasalle, Hugo, 1898–1990. History of Religions. Specialty: The Relationship between Zen Buddhism and Christian Meditation.

Fowler, James: Professor of Practical Theology, Emory University, Atlanta, Georgia. Specialty: Religious Development of Young People.

Gosswoman, Lisa: = Elisabeth Gössmann, theologian, Professor of Philosophy, University of Munich. Specialty: Women's History.

Güstrow, Henneke: = Henneke Gülzow, Professor of Church History and the History of Dogma, Hamburg. Specialties: Ancient Church, Patristics. D. 1997. (N. b.: Güstrow and Gülzow are small towns in the German state of Mecklenburg.)

Heyman, Carter: = Carter Heyward, American feminist theologian. Professor at Episcopal Divinity School, Cambridge, Mass. Specialty: Theology of Relationship.

Hunsbrook, Nicholas H.: = Claus Hunno Hunzinger, Professor of New Testament and Early Judaism, Hamburg. Retired 1992.

Isaias, Joachim: = Joachim Jeremias, Professor of New Testament in the Protestant faculty of theology of the University of Göttingen. Specialties: the historical Jesus, parables research. D. 1979.

Junia: = a woman apostle discovered by feminist exegetes; falsely presented in most editions and translations of Rom 16:7 before 1985 as a man named "Junias."

Köchel, Niklas: = Klaus Koch, Professor of Old Testament and Ancient Oriental Religions, Hamburg. Specialties: Prophets, Daniel, apocalyptic literature. Retired 1989.

Kodaillé, Klaus-Gabriel: = Klaus-Michael Kodalle, Professor of the Philosophy of Religion and Social Ethics, Hamburg; now in Jena. Specialties: Kierkegaard, German Idealism.

McBridges, Reginald and Michaela: = Michael von Brück, Professor of Missiology in the Protestant theological faculty of the University of Munich, and his wife Regine. Specialties: Buddhism in India and Tibet.

Melchior, Hans von: = Hans Urs von Balthasar, influential Swiss Catholic theologian. Specialties: History of salvation in the light of dogma, and its verso: defense of the papacy against contemporary criticism. D. 1988.

Mitscherlight, Alexander: = Alexander Mitscherlich, a psychoanalyst very influential in Germany in the 1960s. Known for his book, *Die vaterlose Gesellschaft*. D. 1982.

Moortown, Nicholas: = Klaus Moersdorf, Professor of Canon Law in the Catholic faculty of theology of the University of Munich. D. 1989.

Najowski, Bertold: = Bernd Janowski, Professor of Old Testament and Ancient Oriental Religions, Hamburg; now in the Protestant theological faculty of the University of Tübingen. Specialties: History and Theology of Atonement.

Northern, Edward: = Edward Noort, Professor of Old Testament and Biblical Archaeology, Hamburg; now in Groningen, Netherlands. Specialties: Archaeology of Israel, Qumran.

Oakes, Wolf-Volkhart: = Wulf-Volker Lindner. Psychoanalyst and Professor of Practical Theology, Hamburg. Specialty: Pastoral Practice.

Petersen, P. Henning: = Henning Paulsen, Professor of New Testament and Early Christianity. Specialty: New Testament literary criticism. D. 1995.

Piscator, Hermann: = Hermann Fischer, Professor of Systematic Theology, Hamburg. Specialties: Friedrich Schleiermacher, Ernst Troeltsch. Retired 1998.

Pitcherhost, Matthäus: = Matthias Kroeger, Professor of Church History and the History of Theology, Hamburg. Specialties: Modern period and twentieth century. Retired 1998.

Ratzeburg, Clemens Cardinal: = Joseph Cardinal Ratzinger, Prefect of the Congregation for the Doctrine of the Faith in the Roman Curia. Formerly Professor of Dogmatic Theology in the Catholic faculty of theology at the University of Regensburg and Archbishop of Munich.

Read, Bernhold: = Bernhard Lohse, Professor of Church History and the History of Dogma, Hamburg. Specialties: Martin Luther and the Reformation, Augustine. D. 1997. Reference is made to his essay, "Die Entscheidung der Lutherischen Reformation über den Umfang des alttestamentlichen Kanons," in idem, *Evangelium in der Geschichte. Studien zu Luther und der Reformation* (Göttingen: Vandenhoeck & Ruprecht, 1988) 211–36.

Redfern, Corinna: = Corinna Dahlgruen, Assistant in the Department of Church History, Hamburg. Doctorate received under the direction of Bernhard Lohse. Now teacher at a college preparatory school in Göttingen.

Redhill, Fulbert: = Wolfgang Grünberg, Professor of Practical Theology, Hamburg. Specialties: Catechesis, Urban Ecclesiology.

Schüssling-Firenze, Elisabeth: = Elisabeth Schüssler Fiorenza, Krister Stendahl Professor of New Testament, Harvard Divinity School, Cambridge, Mass. Specialty: Feminist Exegesis.

Scratch, Timothy: = Tim Schramm, Professor of New Testament, Hamburg. Specialties: New Testament and Judaism, Christian-Jewish dialogue, Feminist Exegesis.

Seeland, Olaf: = Olaf Schumann, Professor of Religion and Missiology, Hamburg. Specialties: Islam and Buddhism in Indonesia.

Short, Jolly: = Ernst Lange, influential in German Protestant Practical Theology. D. 1974.

Sky, Fulko Steven: = Fulbert Steffensky, Protestant practical theologian and teacher of religion in Hamburg (and the husband of Dorothee Sölle). Specialty: Proclamation of the faith in the contemporary political and social context. Retired 1998.

Solo, Dorothea: = Dorothee Sölle, theologian and woman of letters, Professor at Union Theological Seminary, New York; Lecturer in Practical Theology, Hamburg. Retired.

Stampa, Dino: = Dino Staffa, former Professor of Canon Law, Lateran University, Rome. Known for his advocacy of the retention of Latin in the liturgy.

Troll, Thaddäus: German author and satirist. D. 1980.

Vougenot, François: = François Vougat, Professor of New Testament at the University of Lausanne (Switzerland). Specialty: Parables of Jesus in light of literary criticism.

Wild, Egbert: = Eckhart Rau, Professor of New Testament, Hamburg. Specialties: Historical Jesus, Early Church.